Vocabulary and Second Language Writing

The Michigan Series on Teaching Multilingual Writers

Series Editors
Diane Belcher (Georgia State University) and
Jun Liu (SUNY–Stony Brook)

Available titles in the series

Treatment of Error in Second Language Student Writing, Second Edition
Dana R. Ferris

Peer Response in Second Language Writing Classrooms, Second Edition
Jun Liu & Jette G. Hansen Edwards

Critical Academic Writing and Multilingual Students
A. Suresh Canagarajah

Controversies in Second Language Writing:
Dilemmas and Decisions in Research and Instruction, Second Edition
Christine Pearson Casanave

Connecting Reading & Writing in Second Language
Writing Instruction, Second Edition
Alan Hirvela

Genre and Second Language Writing
Ken Hyland

Teacher Written Commentary in Second Language Writing Classrooms
Lynn M. Goldstein

Connecting Speaking & Writing in Second Language Writing Instruction
Robert Weissberg

Technologies in the Second Language Composition Classroom
Joel Bloch

Assessment in the Second Language Writing Classroom
Deborah Crusan

Journal Writing in Second Language Education
Christine Pearson Casanave

Intercultural Rhetoric in the Writing Classroom
Ulla Connor

Genre and Graduate-Level Research Writing
An Cheng

Vocabulary and Second Language Writing
David Hirsh

Vocabulary and Second Language Writing

David Hirsh

University of Sydney

The Michigan Series on Teaching Multilingual Writers

Published in the United States of America
The University of Michigan Press
Manufactured in the United States of America

ISBN-13: 978-0-472-03868-8 (print)
ISBN-13: 978-0-472-12948-5 (ebook)

2024 2023 2022 2021 4 3 2 1

Series Editor Foreword

Those of us who have taught second language writing have probably had the experience of working with students who wish we would devote more class time to helping them expand their vocabularies and whose faces light up when we do. Yet, it is also likely that experienced L2 writing teachers have felt there is never enough time to cover all that the curriculum already requires and who, as a result, view vocabulary as, essentially, icing on the cake, to be added when the cake's rhetorical and syntactic structural components are well in hand. Some number of us may also assume that vocabulary is best addressed in the context of formal reading instruction or that it will just naturally take care of itself through self-sponsored extensive reading.

In his new volume on vocabulary in the L2 writing classroom, David Hirsh, whose decades-long work as a teacher, teacher-educator, and researcher has focused on L2 vocabulary, compellingly persuades us that vocabulary should be seen as a necessary component of L2 writing proficiency and L2 writing instruction, and that we can effectively assess and address L2 writers' vocabulary needs. In this very reader-friendly book, Hirsh offers both a theory-informed and pedagogically oriented state-of-the-art overview of what all of us who are interested in facilitating the learning of L2 writing should know: from why vocabulary size matters to what impact context has, how productive use of vocabulary can be scaffolded, and how technology can support us as teachers and our students as more autonomous learners of vocabulary.

Whether one is new to vocabulary research and pedagogy or already immersed in it, teaching younger learners or adults pursuing advanced degrees, a novice in language and literacy education or a seasoned L2 writing specialist and teacher-researcher, readers of this volume will not only likely find it highly engaging and accessible but also find themselves instilled with a new or greatly renewed appreciation of the role of vocabulary, and of teachers of vocabulary, in the development of L2 writers.

Diane Belcher
Georgia State University

Acknowledgments

I would like to thank the many people who have influenced my thinking on the topic of this book. Key among these are the researchers, teachers and students at the Research Institute for Languages and Cultures of Asia (RILCA) at Mahidol University (Salaya, Thailand), the Research Center for Applied Perceptual Science (ReCAPS) at Kyushu University (Fukuoka, Japan), the English Language Institute (ELI) at Victoria University of Wellington (New Zealand), and the Sydney School of Education and Social Work (SSESW) at the University of Sydney. Many of the activities appearing in this volume have been informed from my time spent in these educational settings. I am especially indebted to Diane Belcher and Jun Liu, the series editors, for affording me the opportunity to write this book and to Kelly Sippell at the University of Michigan Press for her support and guidance with this project.

Grateful acknowledgment is given to the following publishers for permission to reprint previously published materials:

Cambridge University Press for figure of VKS Elicitation Scale by Paribakht & Wesche in *Second Language Acquisition,* copyright © 1997, p. 180; for figure on What is involved in knowing a word by Paul Nation in *Learning Vocabulary in Another Language,* copyright © 2001, p. 27.

Cengage Learning (Houghton Mifflin) for the writing paragraphs activity and Vocabulary Error Code System table in Chapter 15 of *Academic Vocabulary Writing Activities* by Averil Coxhead, copyright 2006, pp. 128 and 130.

Elsevier for Table 1 from "As can be seen: Lexical bundles and disciplinary variation" by Ken Hyland in *English for Specific Purposes,* copyright © 2008, p. 7; Table 4 of SVL in "Advancing disciplinary literacy through English for academic purposes" by C. Greene and J. Lambert in *Journal of English for Academic Purposes,* copyright © 2018, pp. 111–112; for Figures 2 and 3 in "An affix acquisition order for EFL learners" by M. Mochizuki and K. Aizawa in *System,* copyright © 2000, pp. 298–299.

John Wiley & Sons for physical property and chemical property activities by Ash, Lofts, & Evergreen in *Jacaranda Science 2,* copyright © 1998, p. 28; for tables of elementary-level Latin and Greek roots and affixes in "The Latin-Greek connection" by T.V. Rasinski, N. Padak, J. Newton, and E. Newton in *The Reading Teacher,* copyright © 2011, p. 136.

Selami Ok of the Pamukkale University (Turkey) for student experiences on portfolio writing published in *English Language Teaching,* copyright © 2014, p. 58.

Oxford University Press for Appendix 1 of word families by Bauer and Nation in *International Journal of Lexicography,* copyright © 1993, pp. 270–271.

Sage for Academic vocabulary test item in "Developing and exploring the behaviour of two new versions of the Vocabulary Levels Test" by Norbert Schmitt, Diane Schmitt, and Caroline Clapham in *Language Testing,* copyright © 2001, p. 34.

Taylor & Francis for portions from Appendix A in "The development of ESL writing quality and lexical proficiency" by Hyung-Jo Yoon in *Language Assessment Quarterly,* copyright © 2000, p. 402.

The University of Sydney for the excerpt on hydrogen fuel from a Faculty of Engineering Practice Manual, copyright © 2007, p. 7.

Darrell Wilkinson of Tampere University (Finland) for student comments on the use of bilingual word cards published in *TESL-EJ,* copyright © 2017, pp. 6–7.

Every effort has been made to contact the copyright holders for permission to reprint borrowed material. We regret any oversights that may have occurred and will rectify them in future printings of this book.

Contents

List of Figures xiii

Introduction 1

1. Why Is Vocabulary Important in L2 Writing? 5

Guiding Questions 5
The Number of Words in Written Language 5
The Main Types of Words in Writing 7
Collocations and Lexical Bundles 12
Vocabulary Use and Writing Quality 13
Key Points 14
Tasks and Discussion Questions for Teachers 15

2. What It Means to Know and Use a Word 16

Guiding Questions 16
A Model of Vocabulary Knowledge 16
Breadth of Vocabulary Knowledge 17
Depth of Vocabulary Knowledge 19
Mapping Meaning onto Form 20
Word Parts 22
Network Building 27
The Partial-Precise Continuum 28
Key Points 29
Sample Activities for the Classroom 30
Tasks and Discussion Questions for Teachers 32

3. Contextual Differences in Vocabulary Use 33

Guiding Questions 33
Contextual Differences 33
General Service and Technical Words 35

Academic Vocabulary 37
Identifying the Vocabulary Needs of L2 Writers 39
Disciplinary Vocabulary Lists 40
Effect of Context on Collocations 43
Lexical Bundles 44
Use of Word Lists 45
Key Points 46
Sample Activities for the Classroom 47
Tasks and Discussion Questions for Teachers 51

4. Measuring Vocabulary Use in Writing **52**
Guiding Questions 52
Why Measure Vocabulary Size and Knowledge? 52
Approaches to Measuring Vocabulary 53
Measuring Vocabulary Use in L2 Writing 55
Measuring Use of Collocations and Lexical Bundles 65
Teacher Judgments of Lexical Quality in Writing 66
Key Points 67
Tasks and Discussion Questions for Teachers 67

5. Encouraging and Improving Productive Use of Words **68**
Guiding Questions 68
How Words Are Acquired for Productive Use 69
Incidental and Direct Vocabulary Learning 71
The Reading-Writing Connection 77
Conditions Favoring Vocabulary Learning 78
Key Points 84
Sample Activities for the Classroom 85
Tasks and Discussion Questions for Teachers 87

6. Treatment of Errors in Vocabulary Use **88**
Guiding Questions 88
The Nature of Vocabulary Errors 88
Causes of Vocabulary Errors 89
Types of Vocabulary Errors Appearing in Student Writing 91
Errors with Collocations and Lexical Bundles 93
Feedback on Vocabulary Use in Writing 94
Key Points 97
Tasks and Discussion Questions for Teachers 98

7. Technological Applications **99**
Guiding Questions 99
Considerations on the Use of Technology 99
Corpora 100
Building Your Own Corpus 103
Web-Based Resources 104
Software Programs 106
Baseword Lists 107
Concordancing and Collocation Clusters 108
Data-Driven Learning 109
Key Points 112
Tasks and Discussion Questions for Teachers 113

8. Fostering Independent Learning of Vocabulary **114**
Guiding Questions 114
Understanding Autonomous Learning 115
Approaches to Independent Learning of Vocabulary 119
A Role for Translanguaging and the L1 122
Key Points 125
Sample Activities for the Classroom 126
Tasks and Discussion Questions for Teachers 128

References **129**

Index **143**

List of Figures

Figure 1.1: A Sample Engineering Text 8
Figure 1.2: Lexical Coverage of 2,000 High-Frequency Words 9
Figure 1.3: Frequency of Ecology Words in the BNC/COCA Word Lists 11
Figure 1.4: Incorrect and Correct Collocations 12
Figure 2.1: Vocabulary Knowledge Framework 18
Figure 2.2: Word Parts with Meanings and Example Words 23
Figure 2.3: Word Parts with Greek and Latin Forms 24
Figure 2.4: Levels of Affixes 26
Figure 2.5: Affix Order of Acquisition 28
Figure 3.1: Technical Words in Subject Areas 36
Figure 3.2: Most Frequently Occurring Extension Science Words 42
Figure 3.3: Academic Lexical Bundles 45
Figure 4.1: Test Item from Vocabulary Levels Test 53
Figure 4.2: Vocabulary Knowledge Scale 55
Figure 4.3: Vocabulary Descriptors 56
Figure 4.4: Student Text on "How Earthquakes Occur" 57
Figure 4.5: TTR Comparison on Three Texts 58
Figure 4.6: Lexical Profile of the Earthquake Text 60

Figure 4.7: Embedding of Academic Words within the BNC/COCA Word Lists 61
Figure 4.8: Lexical Profile of Text Based on the BNC/COCA 1-10 62
Figure 4.9: Student Text on "My Family" 63
Figure 4.10: Lexical Profile of Text Based on Kids-250 Word Lists 64
Figure 5.1: The Lexical Window for Learning Words in Context 74
Figure 5.2: Input-Based and Task-Based Effects 75
Figure 5.3: Controlled Writing Task 78
Figure 5.4: Experiences with Portfolio Writing in the Words of Students 82
Figure 6.1: Types of Lexical Errors in Writing 92
Figure 6.2: Sample Chart of Vocabulary Error Codes 95
Figure 6.3: Student Text with Lexical Errors Marked for Correction 96
Figure 7.1: Sample VocabProfile Data for a Student Essay 106
Figure 7.2: Examples of Word Family Listings in Baseword Lists 107
Figure 7.3: Items in Kids01 to Kids09 Word Lists 107
Figure 7.4: Concordance Lines for *protect* and *prevent* 108
Figure 8.1: Word Card for *domestic* 119
Figure 8.2: Student Comments on Use of Bilingual Word Cards 120
Figure 8.3: Sample Vocabulary Log with Entry for *succeed* 121

Introduction

Why Writing Teachers Should Care about Vocabulary

More than 40 years ago, Richards (1976) commented on the apparent neglect of vocabulary among scholars and teachers in the field of second language teaching. Since then, there has been a steady increase in interest among researchers and classroom teachers in the contribution of vocabulary knowledge to language use in general. While much of this focus has been on the link between reading and vocabulary in terms of the role of reading in vocabulary learning and in terms of the importance of vocabulary knowledge when reading, there has not been comparable interest in the role of vocabulary in writing. This is reflected in the observation made by Folse (2010, 2020) that vocabulary is widely viewed as the responsibility of the reading teacher although what actually happens in the language classroom is shaped by teacher preferences.

Where do we stand with regard to our understanding of the role of vocabulary in writing, and why should writing teachers be concerned about the vocabulary knowledge of their L2 learners? A useful way to approach these related questions is to consider the centrality of writing in second language learning. We can think of this in terms of writing development in early childhood and elementary school programs, where literacy development in the **L1** (i.e., the first language or mother tongue) informs literacy development in the **L2** (i.e., the second, foreign, or additional language). As learners build up their understanding of the world and accumulate vocabulary knowledge needed to express their ideas and understanding, the link between vocabulary knowledge and writing is apparent. Put simply, without words, language cannot be produced, and the more words one knows, the greater the scope for discussing ideas in writing with detail and sophistication.

As students progress into secondary school and beyond into tertiary study and working life, important words associated with specific areas of the syllabus, academic disciplines, and professional life need to be acquired. These technical words allow for subject-specific discussion of ideas. In addition, academic words can provide a subject-independent framework for tertiary students to present ideas in their writing.

Writing teachers have a central role to assume in shaping attitudes toward vocabulary in the writing class. They can guide students with building up knowledge of words that will enhance the quality of writing; they can provide their learners with activities and tasks that scaffold the process of introducing newly acquired words into writing; and they can provide feedback on the accuracy and appropriateness of word choice. Teachers can also introduce their learners to online resources that can play a role in vocabulary development and guide their students with independent learning of words for use in writing.

The Purpose of This Book

The purpose of this book is to provide writing teachers with principled approaches to focusing on vocabulary in second language writing, with appreciation of the differing contexts for writing and how that affects vocabulary needs and use. In preparing the book, considerations were given to the changing field of language teaching and the ways that emerging ideas may shape how existing and new L2 writing teachers interact with the ideas addressed in the book's chapters. The field of language teaching has seen a shift in language teaching pedagogy toward a **post-method era** (Kumaravadivelu, 2006), where it is no longer deemed appropriate for a set methodology to be adopted in a teaching context without appreciation for the specific needs, values, and beliefs of teachers and students. We have seen a shift, particularly in bilingual and multilingual education research, toward embracing a multiplicity of languages in the L2 classroom, involving a breaking down of traditional barriers between languages to create a space for **translanguaging** (García, 2013), in which the full linguistic repertoire of students is valued and utilized. Ortega (2013) talks of a **bilingual/multilingual turn** in second language teaching, which takes more account of the languages students bring with them into the language classroom. This shift removes imbalances in power and the marginalization of community and indigenous languages stemming from decades of discriminatory language policy and practice (Spolsky, 2007). We are seeing writing viewed in its disciplinary and social context, with ideas about writing across the disciplines, taking hold in L2 writing pedagogy. This recognizes the impact of social setting on the nature of and expectations of writing. Belcher (2012) highlights the **context-bound** nature of writing, suggesting the need for views of L2 writing to be sensitive to the setting in which it occurs and specifically to the knowledge, experiences, and aspirations of the writer. This book seeks to anticipate the theoretical and pedagogical world in which L2 writing teachers will engage with their learners in the process of writing development in the coming years.

Organization of the Book

The book presents a range of perspectives on vocabulary use in L2 writing through the eight chapters that cover: why vocabulary is important to L2 teachers (Chapter 1), what it means to know and use words (Chapter 2), how context shapes word use (Chapter 3), the ways of measuring word use in writing (Chapter 4), approaches to encouraging and enhancing word use in writing (Chapter 5), treatment of vocabulary errors in writing (Chapter 6), technological applications with vocabulary (Chapter 7), and fostering learner autonomy (Chapter 8). The chapters conclude with key points arising from the discussion and tasks and discussion questions for teachers. Sample activities that can be used in primary/elementary school, secondary school, and tertiary settings are included in the book in select chapters that have a strong classroom teaching focus embedded in the discussion (Chapters 2, 3, 5, and 8). I hope that the book serves as a discussion piece for teachers to come to their own informed understandings of how they wish to shape teaching and learning behaviors among their multilingual writers with regard to vocabulary use.

Chapter 1

Why Is Vocabulary Important in L2 Writing?

GUIDING QUESTIONS

1. What is known about the vocabulary size of L2 writers?
2. Which words are the most useful for multilingual writers?
3. How does vocabulary use affect L2 writing quality?

This chapter explores the role that vocabulary takes on in written language, in a general sense, as a starting point for understanding the process of incorporating a vocabulary focus in the L2 writing classroom with sensitivity to our students' learning contexts, which later chapters address. The discussion first looks at what is known about the number of words appearing in written language, the main types of words used, and the role of collocations and lexical bundles in writing, and then moves on to the relationship between vocabulary use and L2 writing quality.

The Number of Words in Written Language

A useful starting point for thinking about what words L2 writers need to know and use is to consider the number of words used in written language. One approach we could use for determining this is to estimate the number of words in contemporary English. We have a reliable estimate that there are 114,000 words in contemporary English, based on a well-principled count of dictionary entries (Goulden, Nation, & Read, 1990). What do we know about this number? First, it represents groupings of words with similar form and meaning into **word families**. To illustrate this, consider some word family members for *help*: *helps, helped, helping, helpful,* and *unhelpful.* These are commonly used, regular and salient in terms of form, and thus can be regarded as closely related from a language learning perspective (Bauer & Nation, 1993). As such, their appearances in the dictionary were counted as repetitions of the same word family. Second, many of the words in the dictionary are not commonly used in the language. Third, some words have a general purpose, while others are highly specialized and technical in nature, or even archaic. The relevant point here for us is that some words are more useful than others for L2 writers.

Another approach to determining the number of words used in written language is to estimate the vocabulary size of well-educated adult native speakers who have experienced 12 years of schooling. Goulden, Nation, and Read (1990) found that L1 university students know around 17,000 word families. This number was not based on measures of written language and may not reflect the vocabulary typically used in their writing. It does, however, capture the words native speakers have been exposed to and have internalized in their mental lexicon. This number roughly equates to 1,000 new words acquired for each year of schooling, corresponding to two or three new words acquired each day. A key element of the process of L1 vocabulary acquisition is the opportunity to meet words repeatedly in new contexts over time, and with sensitivity to form and meaning. The process is "slow but sure."

A third approach that could be used for determining the number of words used in written language is to examine how many appear in specific types of written texts. If we look at senior high school level textbooks in the pure and social sciences, we discover that 16,000 words are used

(Matsuoka & Hirsh, 2018). This figure similarly counts words as word families. It is much lower than the 114,000 words in contemporary English. However, it is close to the 17,000 words known by educated native speakers, suggesting a close relationship between words appearing in school textbooks and words acquired during schooling. If the 16,000–17,000 number is used as a rough estimate of the core number of words known by sophisticated language users, then we need to recognize that there are additional specialist areas of language that have their own specialized vocabularies, such as in aviation, banking, and industrial chemistry, to name just a few. Thus, it is useful to consider both core vocabulary and specialized vocabularies when considering words used in writing.

What is known about the vocabulary knowledge of L2 students? Studies in foreign and second language contexts describe learners of English with considerably smaller vocabulary sizes than 16,000–17,000 words. For example, Miralpeix and Muñoz (2018), measuring vocabulary knowledge in a participant group of 42 Catalan/Spanish students in their first year of undergraduate studies, found vocabulary sizes ranging from 2,500–7,200 words, with an average of 5,100 words. Lower numbers are also reported in Milton, Wade, and Hopkins' (2010) study of 30 L2 students in U.K. pre-sessional programs preparing for undergraduate and graduate studies, finding an average vocabulary size for their participant group of 2,844 words. When considering the number of words required for L2 writers, attention then shifts to which words will provide the best value for learning effort in terms of contributing to effective writing.

The Main Types of Words in Writing

To explore the main types of words appearing in writing, let's look at a short sample of writing (see Figure 1.1) appearing in a university engineering textbook and discussing generation of hydrogen fuel (University of Sydney, 2007).

Figure 1.1: A Sample Engineering Text

Hydrogen fuel

The hydrogen used as fuel in a fuel cell can be derived from various sources including:

1. Electrolysis of water
2. Gasification of biomass
3. Catalytic cracking of crude oil fractions

In this study, we will examine electrolysis of water as a means of generating hydrogen.

Source: University of Sydney, 2007, p. 7. Used with permission.

Figure 1.1 shows three types of words. The first type of words are **general service** words (also termed **high-frequency** words). These include: *the, used, as, in, a, can, be, from, various, including, cracking, of, water, oil, this, study, we, will, examine, means.* These words appear in all forms of writing and provide good return for learning effort. For this reason, they are regarded as a core vocabulary for L2 students.

The second type of words in Figure 1.1 are **academic** words (sometimes called **sub-technical**). There are three occurrences of academic words in this sample: *derived, sources, generating.* Academic words are more associated with academic writing than other forms of writing, such as novels or news stories, and are thus considered specialized within academic contexts of language use. These words represent around 10 percent of word occurrences in academic writing across a range of subject areas and so represent an important component of vocabulary knowledge for students on an academic pathway.

The third type of words in this sample are **technical** words. These include: *hydrogen, fuel, cell, electrolysis, gasification, biomass, catalytic, crude, fractions.* Since the text in Figure 1.1 concerns engineering, many words are included that are specific to discussions of technical concepts in engineering. These words are specialized to this subject area, occurring much more frequently in this particular sample than would be the case in representative writing in other domains such as banking, sports, or the arts.

Let's look at the three types of words in more detail. West (1953) grouped together the 2,000 most frequently occurring words in written language, with consideration to including words that offer the best list for general use, to form the **General Service List (GSL)** of English words. These high-frequency words provide good coverage—that is, they account for a large proportion of word occurrences—in a range of text types (see Figure 1.2).

For some research and pedagogical purposes, the 2,000-word list is separated into two lists of 1,000 words termed **K1** (first 1,000) and **K2** (second 1,000), to take account of the substantially higher text coverage of K1 words when compared to K2 words.

Aside from general service words, there has been considerable interest for many decades in capturing the sub-technical or academic vocabulary appearing in scholarly texts. Starting with initial attempts to document words being translated by L2 students when exposed to English textbooks (see Lynn, 1973), the focus has shifted to identifying words beyond the GSL that are commonly used in a wide range of academic disciplines. Words such as *evidence, method, role, identify, specify, global, domestic,* and *supplementary* do not hint at the subject matter being discussed. Rather, they help to describe the process or activities that academic writers or researchers employ to construct or discuss ideas. In this sense, they are **subject-independent**. An independently created list, the **Academic Word List (AWL),** groups together 570 subject-independent word families appearing in the arts, commerce, law and science,

Figure 1.2: Lexical Coverage of 2,000 High-Frequency Words

Study	Text Type	Lexical Coverage
Hirsh & Nation (1992)	children's fiction	90%
Hwang & Nation (1989)	newspaper stories	80%
Coxhead (2000)	academic texts	76%
Matsuoka & Hirsh (2010)	an EFL course book	90%

representing on average 10 percent of all word occurrences in academic writing (Coxhead, 2000). For L2 students preparing for college or university study, academic words provide a lexical framework that can help them to present specialized ideas in their writing.

There is also considerable research interest in exploring subject-related or **technical** vocabulary appearing in texts. These words are central to a discussion of the chosen subject and would appear frequently in such writing. In this sense, they are **subject-dependent**. In a writing task about family, for example, students may consider using words such as *parent, child, sister, brother, relative, cousin, uncle, aunt, niece* and *nephew*, as these are closely related to the subject area. These words in the general lexicon can thus assume a subject-related purpose. Some subject areas have highly specialized vocabulary in the sense that they are much more likely to appear in writing in the subject area than in other texts. For example, words such as *acceleration, force, friction, inertia, motion,* and *velocity* have been identified as specifically associated with physics (Ardasheva & Tretter, 2017) and appear much more frequently in physics texts than in the general language.

Two additional groups of words deserve mention. One group of words in written language that has received attention is **proper nouns**, or the names of people and places (*Martha, Paris, Lake Victoria*). In narratives and news stories, these words can form a central character thread through the writing. Hirsh and Nation (1992) were of the view that these words seldom present L2 students with a vocabulary learning burden because their meaning is either built up in the story development, as in the case with character development in Harry Potter novels, or activated through prior knowledge of the words through reference to known people or place names.

Texts may also include **low-frequency** words to provide a sense of style or color to the writing. These infrequently occurring words, such as *serendipity, cacophony, erudite,* and *ubiquitous*, are not typically the focus of a vocabulary learning program due to the poor return they provide for learning effort.

One question is where general service words end and specialized vocabulary items begin. Looking beyond the 2,000 general service words, the value of learning effort drops markedly, to the extent that direct teaching of non-specialist words beyond the third 1,000 words is not common. Words at the third 1,000 level, the fifth 1,000 level, and the tenth 1,000 level have been used in combination with the GSL and a list of university words to measure receptive vocabulary knowledge (Nation, 1983), as well as controlled productive vocabulary knowledge (Laufer & Nation, 1999). More recently, Paul Nation has constructed word frequency lists in groups of 1,000 words based on the British National Corpus (BNC) and the Corpus of Contemporary American English (COCA). These BNC/COCA word lists provide a sensitive picture of the distribution of words in the language at a range of frequency levels, as illustrated with distribution of ecology words in the BNC/COCA lists (see Figure 1.3).

The important take-away from this discussion of types of words in written texts is that the criteria of frequency and specialization allow for words to be viewed in relation to their importance in the language.

Figure 1.3: Frequency of Ecology Words in the BNC/COCA Word Lists

BNC/COCA Word Frequency Level	Words
1,000	*cat, dog, horse, rabbit*
2,000	*environment, fox, fur, wool*
3,000	*vision*
4,000	*habitat, butterfly, mammal, owl, predator, prey*
5,000	*ant, coral, mosquito, niche, pigeon, spider*
6,000	*aquatic, camel, ecosystem, glacier, lizard, oyster, squirrel, wasp*
7,000	*amphibian, badger, hoof, reptile, snail, terrestrial*
8,000	*canine, carnivore, otter*
9,000	*mollusk, nocturnal*
10,000	*giraffe*

Collocations and Lexical Bundles

The discussion so far has focused on individual words, which is the central concern of this book. However, in the L2 writing class, teachers will often spend time with their students looking at words that frequently occur together in written language, as semantically related pairs, termed **collocations**, and in larger groupings of three, four, five, and six words, termed **lexical bundles**. The idea of exploring the company that words keep, based on their strong cohesive relations, is becoming well established in the L2 writing literature (Boers & Webb, 2018).

Collocations can be thought of as words that appear together in the language more frequently than chance and more frequently than expected based on their individual frequencies (Durrant, 2009). To illustrate this, *strong* + *coffee* leads to a widely occurring combination much more commonly used than other combinations like *powerful coffee* or *heavy coffee*. In this regard, *strong coffee* is regarded as a collocation and conveys a clear meaning that is not realized with the other two forms.

For Antle (2018), one of the popular motivations for teaching collocations to L2 writers is the idea that collocations can help L2 writers to sound more native speaker–like in their writing. While rules of grammar would allow for a large range of possible collocations, native-speaker writing presents us with those that sound right in terms of usage. Thus, *taking medicine* and *eating medicine* are both grammatically correct, but the latter does not reflect L1 usage (Huang & Tsao, 2019: 3). Some collocations will be closely linked to the writing task topic (see Figure 1.4) and thus could appear in the writing of many students in the class.

Figure 1.4: Incorrect and Correct Collocations

Writing Topic	Incorrect Collocation	Correct Collocation
Paragraph describing gravity	*invent gravity*	*discover gravity*
Essay on the value of part-time employment while at university	*large income*	*high income*

Collocations tend to be distinguished from lexical bundles (also termed **lexical chunks, multiword segments, formulaic sequences**, and **phraseology**) that describe groups of three, four, five, or even six words that have a statistical tendency to co-occur in the language. In other words, they appear frequently (a frequency threshold is applied determining the minimum number of occurrences required in a corpus) and the occurrences are dispersed quite evenly across a range of registers within a corpus (a dispersion threshold is also applied). They also tend to be structurally incomplete, in that they represent only parts of phrases or clauses. To illustrate this, the lexical bundles *as well as*, *has been shown to*, and *is one of the most* form part of larger phrases or clauses in the language. An important distinction needs to be made between lexical bundles, which are semantically transparent (i.e., their meaning is evident from their composition), and idioms, such as *by and large*, *red herring*, and *pull strings*, which are less semantically transparent (i.e., they convey meanings that may only loosely be inferred from their composition and in some cases are semantically opaque based on composition) (Espinal & Mateu, 2010). The advent of corpora and lexical software has enhanced the capacity to explore lexical bundles, most commonly three-word and four-word segments, with an overall pattern of decreasing frequency and dispersion as the number of words in the segment increases.

Vocabulary Use and Writing Quality

Two studies in the 1990s provide some indication of the impact of vocabulary knowledge on writing quality. While investigating 210 L2 writing samples using two L1 ESL teacher ratings, Astika (1993) found that vocabulary accounted for the greatest variance in overall grades awarded using five assessment criteria for writing (content, organization, vocabulary, language use, and mechanics). This is supported by Engber's (1993) finding of strong positive correlations between lexical variation and writing quality. The guideline of "the more, the better" appears to apply when the role of vocabulary in writing quality is considered, although this should be thought of both in terms of quantity of words known and quality of word knowledge.

The interest in focusing on vocabulary use in L2 writing has been shaped by teacher ratings of writing quality, with findings that more proficient writers draw on a larger vocabulary (Schoonen et al., 2011), while lower-proficiency writers tend to over-utilize a small vocabulary (Jarvis, 2013). As the proficiency level of students increases, we would expect to see expansion of the number of words known and a corresponding expansion in the range of words used in writing. This can be described both in terms of the quantity of words known and in the sophistication of words known. The relationship between vocabulary size and writing quality is reflected in the words of Laufer and Nation (1995: 319):

> We can reasonably expect learners' vocabulary size as measured by a vocabulary test to be reflected in the learners' productive use of the language. Where this does not happen, we need to look with concern at the opportunities that the learner has to bring language knowledge into use and adjust the language programme accordingly.

The role of the language program in vocabulary development and vocabulary use in writing is discussed further in Chapter 5.

Key Points

1. There is strong empirical evidence for a vocabulary focus in L2 writing as a means to enhance writing quality.
2. Different types of words are used in writing: general purpose, academic, and technical.
3. As students develop their overall knowledge of the language, they draw on a larger and more sophisticated vocabulary in their writing, contributing to the overall quality of the writing.
4. Beyond individual words, understandings of commonly used collocations and lexical bundles can provide students with a useful resource to further improve the quality of their writing.

Tasks and Discussion Questions for Teachers

1. With language learners described as having a limited knowledge of vocabulary, what would you expect to see in their paragraph writing? Think in terms of text length (number of words), types of words used, repetitions of words, accuracy of words used, and other features of their writing. In light of this, what would you say to a group of students about the importance of building up vocabulary knowledge as a way to improve the quality of their writing?
2. You notice a student learning words from a dictionary, with no apparent discrimination of words. What could you tell this student that would make the learning process more effective?
3. Your students are asking you to teach them collocations, idioms, and lexical bundles to use in their writing because they believe this will make their writing more sophisticated. How would you respond to this request? What considerations would shape your response?

Chapter 2

What It Means to Know and Use a Word

GUIDING QUESTIONS

1. What is the difference between breadth and depth of vocabulary knowledge?
2. Which aspects of vocabulary knowledge are associated with using words in writing?
3. What does it mean to say that vocabulary knowledge moves from partial to precise?

This chapter explores the concepts of breadth and depth of vocabulary knowledge to resolve the dual concerns of quantity and quality of vocabulary knowledge. This leads to an identification and discussion of various aspects of vocabulary knowledge associated with knowing a word deeply. The chapter concludes by considering the concept of "partial-precise knowledge" to show how vocabulary knowledge is incremental.

A Model of Vocabulary Knowledge

Knowing the spelling of words and their core meanings is important for their use in writing, but there are aspects of vocabulary knowledge beyond the form-meaning relationship that affect how L2 learners use words effectively. Nation (2001) presents a model of vocabulary knowledge in terms of **form**, **meaning**, and **use**, distinguishing between vocabulary knowledge used for **receptive** (reading, listening) and **productive** (writing, speaking) skills (see Figure 2.1).

Beyond form and meaning relations, how does one word relate to other words? Words are collectively stored in a **mental lexicon**, and accessing words from the lexicon for use in writing is shaped by a range of concerns:

- What meaning is to be conveyed?
- What are the word choices available, and which is most suited to the writing task?
- How do other words used in the writing affect this choice and the form of word used (i.e., noun, verb, adjective, adverb)?
- Which words tend to occur together in the language (as collocations) that could be used in the writing with good effect?
- How can word choice give the writing a suitable tone (e.g., formal-informal) and meet the expectations of the task and its social setting (i.e., school, workplace, university)?

The L2 writer has many concerns to address when bringing words into writing.

Breadth of Vocabulary Knowledge

We can assume that "more words is better" when it comes to L2 writing, as having a large vocabulary size allows for more choice and precision in the use of words. This view of vocabulary in terms of quantity (**breadth**) of knowledge provides one important perspective on vocabulary use in writing. Studies mapping vocabulary size against writing performance offer some support for the interest in quantity (see, e.g., Milton, 2013; Staehr, 2008; Varnaseri, 2016).

Figure 2.1: Vocabulary Knowledge Framework

Form	Spoken	R	What does the word sound like?
		P	How is the word pronounced?
	Written	R	What does the word look like?
		P	How is the word written and spelled?
	Word Parts	R	What parts are recognisable in this word?
		P	What word parts are needed to express the meaning?
Meaning	Form and Meaning	R	What meaning does this word form signal?
		P	What word form can be used to express this meaning?
	Concepts and Referents	R	What is included in the concept?
		P	What items can the concept refer to?
	Associations	R	What other words does this make us think of?
		P	What other words could we use instead of this one?
Use	Grammatical Functions	R	In what patterns does the word occur?
		P	In what patterns must we use this word?
	Collocations	R	What words or types of words occur with this one?
		P	What words or types of words must we use with this one?
	Constraints on Use (Register, Frequency)	R	Where, when, and how often would we expect to meet this word?
		P	Where, when, and how often can we use this word?

Key: R = receptive knowledge; P = productive knowledge
Source: Nation, 2001, p. 27. Used with permission of Cambridge University Press.

One of the patterns observed in such studies is that the returns for vocabulary learning effort are substantial at the start, as learners build up productive knowledge of the most frequently occurring words in English. The most frequently occurring 2,000 words include important function words such as articles (*the, a, an*), prepositions (*of, in, at, by, between*), auxiliary verbs (*be, do, have*), pronouns (*I, you, she, he, we, they*), and conjunctions (*and, but, so, since, as*). Alongside these function words are commonly used content words—nouns, verbs, adjectives, and adverbs that convey ideas and subject matter. Command over this core vocabulary provides a strong basis for communication in writing, albeit limited in terms of scope for sophisticated or specialized discussion of ideas.

Beyond this core vocabulary lies less commonly used words, and these can add lexical richness to writing. As Johnson, Acevedo, and Mercado (2016) observe in their review of previous research on vocabulary use in writing, "the use of words that appear less frequently in the English language is associated with stronger L2 writing performance as well as L2 writing development over time" (p. 701). Thus, part of the focus for L2 writers is developing a vocabulary of commonly used words and then moving onto effective use of other words that relate to the subject matter and type of writing.

Depth of Vocabulary Knowledge

Another important perspective of vocabulary in writing is the quality (**depth**) of knowledge of words. As knowledge of individual words improves, the scope for their effective use in writing is enhanced. Henriksen (1999) sees depth as reflecting the complex nature of word knowledge, with many components contributing to understanding and representation of a word. There appears to be a **threshold** of knowledge required for a word to be activated in writing (Henriksen & Haastrup, 1998), and this takes our attention to the components of vocabulary knowledge in the depth dimension.

Henriksen (1999) describes vocabulary knowledge through two processes, that convey a sense of depth and complexity that reflect the demands of using a word in writing:

1. developing form-meaning relationships
2. understanding relationships between words

Henriksen (1999) describes the first as a process of mapping meaning onto form, and the latter as a process of network building.

Mapping Meaning onto Form

When mapping meaning onto form, vocabulary use is viewed in terms of the way in which the form of the word activates word meaning. This view of vocabulary use would conceptualize word form as a code, and shared knowledge of this code is what would then allow writing to be meaningful. Thus, the word form *mouse* activates a mental image based on previous experiences. A hundred years ago, this image would consistently be of a small mammal. Today, however, the word form *mouse* could just as easily activate the image of a computer mouse. Thus, the code is **socially constructed** and can change over time. The change over time could be to word form (i.e., spelling) as seen in shifts in preferred spelling over time between *hiccough* and *hiccup*, but would more likely affect word meanings and uses. In addition, L2 writers can update their understanding of the code with exposure to the language, ideally with feedback on accuracy of use, and with exposure to experiences. An understanding of the word form *mammal* can thus evolve for students in preschool or elementary school, with more sophisticated understandings of terrestrial (i.e., land) and aquatic (i.e., fresh water and marine) mammals developing over time. For elementary and high school students, changes could occur with understandings of the word form *pollution* to represent more sophisticated uses over time, including air, land, water, environmental, atmospheric, glacial, noise, and visual pollution. Thus, understanding of word code is shaped by understandings of the world in physical, social, and intellectual ways.

For L2 writers to use words with confidence, they would need familiarity with word spelling. If words are considered to be members of word families, then knowledge of word spelling will evolve as L2 writers develop command over different **parts of speech** (noun, verb, adjective, adverb). It will also evolve as L2 writers develop command over **prefixes** (*re-, sub-, anti-, un-*) and **suffixes** (*-ly, -ness, -ment*) associated with derived forms of words. Thus, there is considerable pedagogical interest in word form as a separate component of vocabulary knowledge.

However, writing is principally about conveying ideas, so it's common to look at writing as a process of mapping meaning onto form, where word form is a tool used to activate meaning. If the code is presented correctly (i.e., correct spelling and word form), then a meaning can be activated. Thus, effective writers use word form to construct meaning. When this process works well, with a collection of words in the form of a text, readers tend not to notice individual words as word forms but rather experience them as meanings. However, when word form is faulty, the reader's attention is taken to word form, as a step in the process of trying to decipher the code.

The process of mapping meaning onto form is shaped by complexities with word meaning, as many words have multiple meanings. **Polysemy** refers to multiple meanings of a word—*bright* can mean "shining" and "intelligent." With polysemy, some meanings will be more useful or relevant than others. Thus, the term *issue* can mean "a person's lineal descendants including their children" in legal studies, but this meaning is rarely used outside of legal contexts.

Word Parts

Some languages have transparent relationships between word form and meaning. In Semitic languages, such as Arabic and Hebrew, word roots made up of three (and occasionally four) consonants convey a meaning. Within a Semitic language, several thousand roots, each with a corresponding core meaning, can be shaped into nouns, verbs, adjectives, and/or adverbs using a small number of templates. Collectively, the small number of templates and large number of word roots provide the language with a high degree of **semantic transparency** (Shimron, 2003).

While English was originally a Germanic language, there have been influences from French and subsequent borrowing from Latin, Greek, and other languages to equip the language with the lexical resources suited to scholarly writing. These influences on English have given rise to a complicated relationship between form and meaning. The result is that different L2 writers can have different feelings about the ease or difficulty of word learning, based on other languages they know. To illustrate this idea, Baeskow (2006) sheds light on Romance roots adopted in English, such as *duce, scribe, ceive, sume, mit,* and *port.* These roots, when attached to prefixes (such as *re-, in-, per-, con-, ad-, ex-*), give rise to words such as *reduce, inscribe, perceive, consume, admit,* and *export* in which the form-meaning relationship may be relatively transparent to L2 learners with knowledge of Romance languages such as Catalan, French, Italian, Portuguese, Romanian, and Spanish. However, these roots may not be so semantically transparent to L2 writers who lack knowledge of Romance languages.

Some writing teachers may have a particular interest in teaching word parts of English, many derived from Greek and Latin, reflecting patterns of substantial borrowing into English from these two languages for technical and scholarly terms. Figure 2.2 lists a sample of prefixes, word roots (also called *bases*), and suffixes of English with meanings and example words provided.

Figure 2.2: Word Parts with Meanings and Example Words

	Form	Meaning	Example
Prefixes	*co-*	with, together	*coincidence*
	ex-	out	*extract*
	pre-	before	*preview*
	pro-	forward, ahead	*proceed*
	trans-	across	*translate*
Roots	*audi*	hear, listen	*audience*
	cred	believe	*credible*
	dict	say, tell, speak	*dictate*
	graph	write, draw	*graph*
	mobil	move	*mobile*
	port	carry	*transport*
	scrib	script, write	*scribble*
	vis	see	*visible*
Suffixes	*-able*	can	*capable*
	-arium	place for	*aquarium*
	-er	more	*quieter*
	-est	most	*slowest*
	-ful	full of	*successful*
	-ify	to make	*quantify*
	-less	without	*fearless*

Source: Adapted from Rasinski et al., 2011, p. 136. Used with permission by John Wiley & Sons.

There are multiple instances of **parallel forms** in English drawn from Greek and Latin, exemplified in the words *bicycle* and *bilingual* with the Latin *bi-* meaning "two," and the term *carbon dioxide* where the Greek *di-* also refers to "two." Rasinski et al. (2011) list further examples of these Greek-Latin parallel forms (see Figure 2.3).

A related dimension of mapping form onto meaning is the effect of the L1 on L2 processing. For languages that share common roots, as occurs with German and English because of Germanic influences on early English and with French and English because of French influences on English, there may

Figure 2.3: Word Parts with Greek and Latin Forms

	Latin	Greek	Meaning	Examples
Prefixes	*contra-*	*anti-*	against	*contradict, antisocial*
	circu- / circum-	*peri-*	around	*circumference, perimeter*
	multi-	*poly-*	many	*multinational, polygon*
	super- / sur-	*hyper-*	over	*supersonic, hyperactive*
	sub-	*hypo-*	under, below	*submarine, hypothermia*
Bases	*aqua*	*hydro*	water	*aquatic, hydroelectric*
	ped	*pod*	foot, feet	*pedestrian, tripod*
	terr	*geo*	earth	*territory, geographic*

Source: Adapted from Rasinski et al., 2011, p. 136. Used with permission of John Wiley & Sons.

be opportunities for positive transfer of knowledge of words in the L1 to newly met words in the L2. This can facilitate rapid processing of L2 words, as form-meaning relationships are largely transferrable. This can be seen in identical forms in English-French (*patience-patience*; *information-information*) and the strong similarities between *doctor* (English) and *doktor* (German), *garden* (English) and *garten* (German), and *artist* (English) and *artiste* (French). The similarity becomes weaker with *coffee* (English) and *kaffee* (German) and with *identical* (English) and *identique* (French). These are termed **cognates**, with greater transferability of L1 knowledge to the L2 with stronger cognates than with weaker cognates.

This pattern is called **cross-linguistic similarity** (Otwinowska & Szewczyk, 2019). While the similarity can have a positive effect on vocabulary learning in the L2, this is not always the case. Similarity in word form between two languages can lead to wrong assumptions about similarity in meaning. **False cognates** are when two words in different languages have a similar form but different meanings. False cognates can be seen with English and German, where the German *gymnasium* refers to a "grammar school" (and not a "gym"), and with English and French, where the French *grappe* refers to a "bunch" (and not a "grape"). False cognates can have closely associated meanings in the two languages, as in German *see* meaning a "lake" and French *librairie* meaning a "bookshop." However, meanings can also be unrelated in the two languages, as is the case with the German *gift* meaning "poison."

As L2 learners develop their vocabulary knowledge, they will display an increased awareness of the role of **affixes** (prefixes and suffixes) in constructing word meaning. Bauer and Nation (1993) constructed seven levels of derivatives to capture degrees of difference between word forms so that words such as *help-helps* are more likely to be recognized as being in the same word family than is the case with *picture-picturesque*. Level 1 means all forms are treated as new words, while Level 6 allows for very large groupings of words into word families and requires a very complex and sophisticated understanding of the role of prefixes, suffixes, and other inflections in the language (see Figure 2.4).

The first candidates to be included in a word family, representing the easiest learning demands, are at Level 2 as shown in Figure 2.4. This would lead to these word families:

- *happy – happier – happiest* (with *happily*, *unhappy*, and *happiness* added at Level 3)
- *enjoy – enjoys – enjoyed – enjoying* (with *enjoyable* added at Level 3 and *enjoyment* added at Level 4)

Bauer and Nation (1993: 255–256) applied a range of criteria to determine the level at which affixes were placed, including:

- **frequency**: the number of words in which an affix occurs
- **productivity**: the likelihood that the affix will be used to form new words
- **predictability**: the degree of predictability of the meaning of the affix
- **regularity** of the form of the affix.

These criteria provide a useful basis for making decisions on which word forms to teach when introducing students to new vocabulary items. In a study of the relationship between affix knowledge and vocabulary size, Mochizuki and Aizawa (2000) found incremental increases in how many affixes L2 learners

Figure 2.4: Levels of Affixes

Level 1
A different form is a different word. Capitalization is ignored.
Level 2
Regularly inflected words are part of the same family. The inflectional categories are: plural; third-person singular present tense; past tense; past participle; *-ing;* comparative; superlative; possessive.
Level 3
-able, -er, -ish, -less, -ly, -ness, -th, -y, non-, un-, all with restricted uses.
Level 4
-al, -ation, -ess, -ful, -ism, -ist, -ity, -ize, -ment, -ous, in-, all with restricted uses.
Level 5
-age (leakage), -al (arrival), -ally (idiotically), -an (American), -ance (clearance), -ant (consultant), -ary (revolutionary), -atory (confirmatory), -dom (kingdom; officialdom), -eer (black marketeer), -en (wooden), -en (widen), -ence (emergence), -ent (absorbent), -ery (bakery; trickery), -ese (Japanese; officialese), -esque (picturesque), -ette (usherette; roomette), -hood (childhood), -i (Israeli), -ian (phonetician; Johnsonian), -ite (Paisleyite), -let (coverlet), -ling (duckling), -ly (leisurely), -most (topmost), -ory (contradictory), -ship (studentship), -ward (homeward), -ways (crossways), -wise (endwise; discussion-wise), ante- (anteroom), anti- (anti-inflation), arch- (archbishop), bi- (biplane), circum- (circumnavigate), counter- (counter-attack), en- (encage; enslave), ex- (ex-president), fore- (forename), hyper- (hyperactive), inter- (inter-African, interweave), mid- (mid-week), mis- (misfit), neo- (neo-colonialism), post- (post-date), pro- (pro-British), semi- (semi-automatic), sub- (subclassify; subterranean), un- (untie; unburden)
Level 6
-able, -ee, -ic, -ify, -ion, -ist, -ition, -ive, -th, -y, pre-, re-
Level 7
Classical roots and affixes

Source: Bauer & Nation, 1993, pp. 270–271. Used with permission of Oxford University Press.

were familiar with as overall vocabulary size increased. In addition, they found that some affixes are typically acquired before others. From their data, they identified an "order of acquisition" of affixes (see Figure 2.5).

From a teaching perspective, affixes high on the order of acquisition will be the easiest to learn because of their **salience** in the language and also provide the best return for learning effort because of their frequency.

Network Building

Aside from viewing vocabulary use in writing from a form-meaning perspective, it can also be viewed in terms of understanding the relationships between words. Known words are described as a **mental lexicon**. A single word can have semantic relationships with other words within the mental lexicon in different ways.

Words can share a meaning (**synonyms**), such as *far* and *distant* and have opposite meanings (**antonyms**), such as *far* and *near*. A word can be an example of a category represented by another word (**hyponyms**) as in *apple* and *fruit*. Groups of words can also exhibit degrees of meaning on a continuum (**gradation**) as in *crawl, walk,* and *run*. These four categories of lexical relations are termed **paradigmatic** (Haastrup & Henriksen, 2000) and are shaped by relationships in the language. They can be reflected in processes of substitution or choice in word use. For example, in the statement "I added *berries* to my yogurt," *berries* could be substituted with *fruit* or *strawberries*, and the statement could still be true. This process is shaped by paradigmatic understandings.

Thus, while paradigmatic relations reflect patterns evident within the language, the term **syntagmatic** is used to describe relations within the immediate clause or sentence being constructed (Haastrup & Henriksen, 2000). This view is localized to the writing, in that a word is said to have a syntagmatic relationship with other words in the clause or sentence. This can be seen in the collocations a writer might use, such as *strong interest, generous serving, feeble excuse*, and *poor understanding*.

Figure 2.5: Affix Order of Acquisition

Affix Order of Acquisition	
Prefixes	**Suffixes**
re-	*-ation*
un-	*-ful*
pre-	*-ment*
non-	*-ist*
anti-	*-er*
semi-	*-ize*
ex-	*-al*
en-	*-ly*
post-	*-ous*
inter-	*-ness*
counter-	*-ism*
in-	*-able*
ante-	*-less*
	-ish
	-y
	-ity

Source: Adapted from Mochizuki & Aizawa, 2000, pp. 298–299. Used with permission of Elsevier.

Haastrup and Henriksen (2000) describe **network building** as a process of lexical progression "where the organisational links in the mental lexicon are strengthened" (p. 222). It is the mapping between words within the mental lexicon that most effectively describes depth of vocabulary knowledge and presents the most demanding and expansive dimensions of vocabulary learning. The network is continuously being updated, as new lexical items are added to the lexicon and as new understandings of words are added.

The Partial-Precise Continuum

The first time L2 learners meet a new word, the process of vocabulary learning commences. However, as instructors, we would not typically expect to see this word appear in L2 learners' writing based on a single meeting because they would only have minimal understanding of the word. At some point, L2 learners would sufficiently understand the form-meaning relationship of this new word to feel confident enough to use it in their writing. The term **frontier words** (see Zareva, 2012) refers to those for which learners have yet to establish strong form-meaning relationships and so the words would not yet be integrated into their existing lexical network. L2 learners can potentially activate and use these words in their writing in the future but, at present, do not sufficiently understand these words for this activation to occur. Repeated meetings of the words in varied contexts will consolidate the learning process.

The process of vocabulary learning progresses along a continuum from partial to precise knowledge (Henriksen, 1999). It starts with noticing the form features of a word and then moves onto understandings of meanings. As students gradually encounter the word in other forms and situations (contexts and with other known words), their ability to use them correctly is improved (Zareva, 2012). In this way, the partial-precise continuum operates with respect both to form-meaning relationships and network building.

Key Points

1. A word is known if a learner can activate word meaning based on word form. Based on this understanding, it's possible to count how many words a learner knows, providing a quantitative representation of vocabulary knowledge in terms of breadth. However, this representation of vocabulary knowledge does not take account of how well a learner knows individual words, both in terms of the understanding of the form-meaning relationship and in terms of the relationship of one word with other words. When we explore the quality of vocabulary knowledge, as opposed to quantity of words known, we are referring to depth of vocabulary knowledge.
2. Vocabulary knowledge is multifaceted, involving understanding of word form and meaning as well as other word aspects. For learners to successfully use a word in writing, they need to activate different aspects of word knowledge. Making a distinction between receptive knowledge, which

refers to recognizing word forms and meanings in written and spoken language, and productive knowledge, which refers to words being produced in spoken or written language, is necessary. In the case of writing, learners need a good understanding of the form-meaning relationship and an awareness of how one word is associated with other words.

3. The process of acquiring word knowledge is incremental. This process begins with the first meetings of a word, resulting in the development of partial knowledge. Frontier words are words learners partially know but cannot yet fully understand or produce. With repeated meetings in meaningful contexts, learners develop a more precise knowledge of these words. At some point, learners meet the threshold of knowledge required for activation and can use the word. Different learners can have different thresholds for activation, and this may be reflected in their accuracy and confidence of vocabulary use in their writing.

Sample Activities for the Classroom

Activity 1: Elementary School Level

In the primary school class, the teacher is introducing forms of transportation. She elicits words from the students (in the L1 or L2) and writes the L2 forms on the board. She then checks that they know the meanings by giving students a task where they match words with pictures of a *bicycle, motorbike, car, van, bus, truck, plane, train,* and *boat.* The students create word cards with the picture on one side and the English word on the other and test each other in pairs to reinforce familiarity with the words and their meanings. The students are then asked to write about the transportation they see in their city, starting with the words: "In my city, there are many forms of transportation."

Activity 2: High School Level

A high school teacher is encouraging her students to build up word family knowledge for some words they use frequently in their writing. These words include nouns (*success, motivation, anxiety, pride, friendship, occupation, society, education)* and verbs (*assist, allow, prevent, protect, restrict, provide, compare, contrast*). The teacher introduces the idea of a vocabulary learning log, where students can record words with meanings and family members. She models one word:

success (n): the achievement of something you plan or attempt to do

succeed (v), *successful* (adj), *successfully* (adv), *unsuccessful* (adj), *unsuccessfully* (adv)

Sentence: *The team <u>unsuccessfully</u> tried to score and lost the game.*

Students are then given five new words each day to add to their logs based on group work and dictionary consultation.

Activity 3: University Level

A writing teacher wishes to apply ideas about teaching word parts (prefixes, suffixes, and word roots) in her L2 writing class to enhance student familiarity with technical vocabulary. Her thinking is that this will improve student knowledge of some of the more problematic words she wants them to use when writing about topics in the social sciences and pure sciences, including *terrestrial, aquatic, portable*, and *audible*. She collates lists with corresponding English meanings of prefixes (*ex-* = out; *re-* = back, again; *multi-* = many), suffixes (*-able* = can; *-est* = most; *-less* = without), and word roots (*audi* = hear; *port* = carry; *terr* = earth) sourced from Rasinski et al. (2011). She assigns students to work in pairs to learn from the lists. This learning is then consolidated with classroom writing activities designed to activate this knowledge. Her students are given a list of target words containing pre-taught prefixes, roots, and suffixes, and asked to include these in a writing task with a related topic. She then provides targeted feedback on the use of the target words.

Tasks and Discussion Questions for Teachers

1. An advanced student dictionary lists words alphabetically with word spellings and meanings provided. It would appear to be a useful resource for learning new words. What concerns would you have if you discovered students attempting to memorize all the words of English from the dictionary, starting from A and working through to Z, as a competition among themselves during the year to see which student could learn English words the fastest?
2. In the case of low-proficiency students, how might the idea of word families be applied in the L2 writing classroom in a way that reflects student familiarity with the language and with affixes (prefixes and suffixes) in particular?
3. Many words in English have multiple meanings (they are polysemous). What principles might be applied in deciding which word meanings to focus on in the context of L2 writing?

Chapter 3

Contextual Differences in Vocabulary Use

GUIDING QUESTIONS

1. What is meant by contextual differences in writing?
2. What effect does context have on vocabulary use?
3. What are subject-dependent and subject-independent words?

This chapter explores the effect of context on word use and focuses on preparing students for academic and occupational life, including English for Academic Purposes (EAP), English for Specific Purposes (ESP), and English for Occupational Purposes (EOP) programs. Next, the chapter looks at general service, technical, and academic words and the development of specialized word lists. The chapter closes with a discussion of how specialized word lists can inform L2 writing pedagogy.

Contextual Differences

L2 writing describes a diverse range of activities in a diverse range of contexts carried out by a diverse population of writers. Multilingual writers include those described as **Generation 1.5** (see Harklau, Lossey, & Siegal, 1999), representing students who arrived in the U.S. at a young age or were born into immigrant families in the U.S. and graduate from U.S. high school still in the process of learning English. The effects of interrupted schooling because of conflict in their home countries, poor English instruction in their home countries, and/or involuntary immersion into English-medium instruction in the U.S. are evident in these students' literacy development; the education system in the U.S. is not always suited to addressing their literacy situation and needs (Belcher, 2012).

Thus, the term *second language* (L2) is convenient but overly simplistic and not always encouraging of a deep investigation of who is involved in writing in another language and how the context of that writing shapes the process and product. As Belcher (2012) notes, writing is highly context bound.

L2 writing occurs at all levels of education (e.g., early childhood, elementary, secondary, undergraduate, graduate) and in academic and professional/occupational settings. Aside from programs of English for general purposes, teaching programs have focused on preparing students for the demands of undergraduate and graduate studies with specialized programs of EAP and ESP such as English for Engineering, English for Business, and English for Nursing. Outside of academic settings, there are EOP programs preparing students for careers in banking, hospitality, and aviation, to name just a few occupational areas. This interest in specialized uses of language has led to a focus on Language for Specific Purposes (LSP). Belcher (2012) highlights the need for more focus on younger L2 learners at primary and secondary school levels, particularly given the challenges facing teachers working with English as an Additional Language (EAL) students in mainstream classrooms.

Within a school, university, or occupational writing program, there are a range of text types (recount, narrative, persuasive, descriptive, poetic, reflective, review, business letter, proposal writing, report writing, essay writing, thesis, and dissertation) and a range of topics (a childhood memory, the water cycle, perspectives on the causes of World War I, providing culturally sensitive patient care in nursing practice). These preceding ideas inform the discussion of context.

General Service and Technical Words

A distinction can be made between vocabulary on the General Service List (GSL)—words appearing frequently in the language in most contexts—and technical vocabulary—words appearing frequently in a specific subject area. While general service words can be used to discuss ideas in a vast range of subject areas, technical words are more constrained in their use. Thus, while *attempt, concern, develop, interest, prepare,* and *situation* could appear in a broad range of subject matters in their role as general service words, these technical words are particularly associated with medical science: *abdominal, inflammatory, antibiotic, immunosuppressive, placebo,* and *vascular.*

General service words can be separated into function words (e.g., *the, of, in, she, he, because, be, do*) and content words (e.g., *sing, agree, child, far, usually*). While the function words do not provide a sense of subject area, it's possible to get a feel for the subject area from some content words. A widely referred to list of general service words is West's (1953) General Service List of 2,000 words. The list is rather dated, though, and does not fully reflect the language of contemporary society given that it includes terms that are less relevant today, including *carriage, ornament, telegraph, solemn,* and *saddle* and does not include contemporary, everyday vocabulary items such as *computer, internet,* and *video.* In response to these concerns about the GSL, researchers have attempted to create new GSLs, including the **NGSL** (Browne, 2014) and the **new-GSL** (Brezina & Gablasova, 2015). These new lists can also be regarded as representations of general service words.

The GSL makes a distinction between the first 1,000 (K1) words and the second 1,000 (K2) words. K1 words are, on average, ten times more likely to be used than K2 words, yet both lists are well worth learning. K1 words are typically acquired first and include words such as *because, child, difficult, increase, people,* and *succeed.* K2 words are generally the next group of words to be acquired and include words like *absence, century, congratulate, excuse, peculiar,* and *sympathy*. There are exceptions to this rule. For example, if a child visits the zoo and sees a giraffe, that word can be acquired even though *giraffe* is not frequently used enough in the language to be included in the GSL.

Technical words are shaped by the subject area being discussed (see Figure 3.1). In chemistry, for example, the terms *reaction, element, bonding, isotope,* and *precipitation* would be frequently used, while in aviation, the terms *runway, terminal, pushback, cockpit,* and *hanger* would be commonly used.

Some general service words may assume technical uses, as in *solution*, which has a general meaning based on the verb *solve* (as in "find a *solution* to the problem"), as well as a technical meaning in chemistry to refer to a liquid with another substance (or substances) dissolved in it (as in "we prepared a saline *solution* of sodium chloride dissolved in H_2O"). Some words may have multiple technical uses in different subject

Figure 3.1: Technical Words in Subject Areas

Subject Area	Most Frequently Occurring Technical Words
Biology	*cell, blood, plant, enzyme, molecule, gene, DNA, protein, body, glucose*
Chemistry	*reaction, acid, ion, atom, form, solution, electron, gas, bond, metal*
Economics	*price, cost, demand, rate, firm, income, goods, market, government, supply*
Geography	*area, country, population, food, river, land, development, city, place, rock*
Mathematics	*find, value, equation, point, line, graph, give, solution, example, area*
History	*war, source, state, world, government, power, party, military, policy, communist*
English	*word, language, say, text, write, writer, think, read, go*
Physics	*energy, force, wave, object, field, current, speed, direction, mass, temperature*

Source: Green & Lambert, 2018, pp. 111–112. Used with permission from Elsevier.

areas. The word *fossilization* has a meaning in archaeology ("preservation in a rock or as a rock") as in *fossilized dinosaur bones,* which differs from the meaning in linguistics ("fixed and unlikely to change") as in *fossilized errors in pronunciation,* although there is a shared core meaning of "a recognizable unchanging pattern shaped by the past" in both these uses.

Academic Vocabulary

If general service words are highly variable in their use and technical words are more constrained, then there is another group of words that falls between these two categories. This is **academic vocabulary.** These words are not generalized enough in the language to be acquired by exposure to general language use and are not usually defined and explained by subject teachers when discussing technical ideas. Therefore, these words could present a considerable challenge to L2 writers.

Studies in the 1970s focused on capturing this academic, or sub-technical, vocabulary in textbooks and other materials that present EFL learners with difficulty (see Campion & Elley, 1971; Ghadessy, 1979; Lynn, 1973; Praninskas, 1972). However, in 2000, Coxhead adopted a fresh approach to the issue, constructing a corpus of texts from 28 subject areas across four disciplinary areas (arts, commerce, law, and science) to provide a representative sample of the types of texts undergraduate students meet at a university. Coxhead (2000) analyzed the corpus of 3.5 million running words to identify the strongest candidates, defined as **word families**, for inclusion in an academic word list based on three criteria (p. 221):

- **specialized occurrence**: words in the GSL were excluded
- **range and uniformity**: words had to occur at least 10 times in each of the four main sections of the corpus and in 15 or more of the 28 subject areas
- **frequency**: words had to occur at least 100 times in the corpus

The result of this work was the **Academic Word List (AWL)**, representing 570 word families and including items like those listed (Coxhead, 2000: 232–235):

analyse	*evaluate*	*modify*
assess	*fluctuate*	*scope*
commodity	*hierarchy*	*simulate*
domestic	*imply*	*specific*
duration	*intrinsic*	*voluntary*

The academic words on this list represent between 8 percent and 12 percent of word occurrences in academic writing. These words alone do not suggest the subject area being discussed and are thus regarded as **subject-independent**.

The development of the AWL can be thought of from two perspectives. First, it can be seen as an attempt to capture or describe language use. In this regard, it has theoretical importance because it helps L2 writers understand the nature of academic writing. Second, it can be seen as an attempt to address a language learning and language use need, making it a pedagogical resource. When viewing academic word lists from a pedagogical (i.e., teaching/learning) perspective, important questions arise:

- How should this list, which has theoretical significance, be applied in practical settings?
- Which words within the list are most useful for L2 writers?
- How will those words be used in different subject areas?

Some academic words have quite stable meanings across different subject areas. These include *data, analyse/analyze,* and *method.* Some academic words such as *isolate* and *violate* may be more shaped in use by subject area. Note how *isolated villages* and *isolate the genome* share a meaning, yet their uses here signal different contextual understandings of the meaning of *isolate*. Similarly, *violate their rights* and *violate the statistical rule* signal rather different uses of *violate*. In the case of the academic word *domestic*, there is a shared common meaning relating to home and country, yet it can be used in legal studies in the context of discussion of *domestic disputes*, in veterinary science in the discussion of *domesticated animals*, in business studies in the discussion of *gross domestic product*, and in sociology in the discussion of *domestic worker conditions*. L2 writing teachers may need to approach different academic words in different ways, some independent of subject area, and some more aligned to their use in specific subject areas (see Hyland & Tse, 2007, for a commentary along these lines).

Such questions have led some researchers to develop specialized lists of academic words. Examples include a nursing academic word list (Yang, 2015) and a medical academic word list (Lei & Liu, 2016), both of which identify words that are collectively more tailored to these subject areas than the AWL is designed or intended to be. When developing the AWL, the range and uniformity criteria used meant that vocabulary items are broadly representative of academic writing across the disciplines.

Identifying the Vocabulary Needs of L2 Writers

L2 writing is a broad term referring to writing at different educational levels; in a range of subject areas, occupational settings, and academic disciplines; covering a range of genres and text types with particular rhetorical structures; and by writers at a range of proficiency levels (Swales, 1990). If researchers can capture the vocabulary of specialized areas of writing, teachers can then tailor vocabulary learning in their L2 writing classroom to suit the writing needs and aspirations of different groups of students. Such a needs-analysis approach accounts for the **present situation** (i.e., the students' current needs and their current performance) and the **target situation** (i.e., the students' future needs) to identify the vocabulary learning gap (St. John & Dudley-Evans, 1998).

The common approach to tailoring vocabulary use for L2 writing students, particularly when focusing on a specific domain of language use, is to build on 2,000 general service words with specialized vocabulary because the specialized words will provide a better return for learning effort than the learning of unspecialized words from the 3,000 word list and beyond. The specialization could be academic words, technical words, or a combination of the two. The focus could be on activating words in the students' existing lexicon as well as introducing new words through reading material with scaffolding as required to promote their productive use (see Chapter 5).

Disciplinary Vocabulary Lists

Researchers have become increasingly interested in capturing the strongest words for inclusion in specialized vocabulary lists for disciplinary areas. This has been facilitated by the construction of large **corpora** (collections of texts in digital form) and the availability of computer programs that can provide a profile of words in a corpus or sub-corpus to enable identification of words based on criteria such as frequency of occurrence, range of texts the word appears in, and uniformity of those occurrences across sections of a corpus.

After what point in vocabulary learning should teachers introduce specialized technical vocabulary? There are various answers to this, reflecting different educational settings and different constraints on the overall language goals of the program. Teachers can introduce technical vocabulary once students have gained:

- familiarity with K1 words
- familiarity with K1 + K2 words
- familiarity with K1 + K2 words and academic words

Ward (2009) wanted to capture words in engineering for lower-level students in an EFL setting. For these students, words in the GSL and the AWL were considered largely unfamiliar, so their appearance in the language of engineering would represent a vocabulary learning demand. Ward consulted the GSL and AWL and excluded function words from his list, including *the, of, is, and, in, a, to, for, that,* and *are* because they would be difficult to teach in the same way as content words and would be acquired naturally through exposure to language. Then he counted all word forms separately rather than in word families, on the assumption that his learners were still developing the required knowledge of the language to recognize word family members. In the end, this is an excerpt from Ward's (2009: 181) resulting list of 299 basic engineering words:

system	*determine*	*process*
equation	*time*	*constant*
value	*figure*	*equations*
flow	*rate*	*function*
data	*force*	*temperature*

Ward's list includes some items from the GSL (i.e., *time, used, given*) and some items from the AWL (i.e., *data, function, analysis*), reflecting his intentions in tailoring a word list for a particular group of learners.

Matsuoka and Hirsh (2018) sought to capture the specialized vocabulary of high school science. They compiled a corpus of 24 published textbooks from Years 11 and 12 (junior and senior years) for biology, chemistry, and physics with 3.9 million running words. It was assumed that some K2 words would appear in the texts as science words. The list thus excluded only K1 words (based on the BNC/COCA) and applied range, frequency, and dispersion criteria to generate a list of 1,012 word families. The most frequent high school science words identified by Matsuoka and Hirsh (2018: 62–63) are shown:

cell	*produce*	*mass*
energy	*atom*	*example*
react	*solution*	*temperature*
acid	*ion*	*metal*
molecule	*electron*	*increase*

In addition, Matsuoka and Hirsh (2018) were interested in identifying words that were excluded from the list due to the range, frequency, and dispersion criteria but could be identified as extension words for biology, chemistry, and physics. The most frequently occurring words in each list are shown in Figure 3.2.

Coxhead and Hirsh (2007) were interested in identifying the strongest candidates for inclusion in a university science word list. They constructed a corpus of complete texts covering 14 undergraduate science subject areas (agricultural science, biology, chemistry, computer science, ecology, engineering and technology, geography, geology, horticultural science, mathematics, nursing and midwifery, physics, sport and health sciences, veterinary and animal sciences) totaling 1.76 million running words. The corpus would be representative of the language of science. They excluded words in the GSL and the AWL and focused on the specialized words of science. They applied the criteria of frequency, range, and dispersion to identify the strongest candidates in this way:

- **frequency**: words occur at least 50 times in the corpus
- **range**: words occur in at least 7 of the 14 subject areas
- **dispersion**: words have a dispersion factor of at least 35

Figure 3.2: Most Frequently Occurring Extension Science Words

Biology	Chemistry	Physics
species	*dissolve*	*volt*
gene	*soluble*	*velocity*
chromosome	*ammonia*	*momentum*
enzyme	*mole*	*mirror*
bacterium	*carbonate*	*physics*
ecosystem	*hydroxide*	*photon*
hormone	*sulfur/sulphur*	*telescope*
mammal	*oxidation*	*vector*
female	*ethanol*	*generator*
allele	*precipitate*	*diode*

Source: Matsuoka & Hirsh, 2018, pp. 65–69.

The research team applied the principle of **word families** (meaning that they counted occurrences of *cell* and *cells* together). The resulting list (Coxhead & Hirsh, 2007: 78) of 318 words includes these items:

acid	*extinct*	*parasite*
cell	*gravity*	*saline*
condense	*hemisphere*	*spatial*
contaminate	*inherit*	*species*
enzyme	*membrane*	*specimen*

New specialist word lists will continue to be developed, as researchers, teachers, and even students look for ways to inform vocabulary use in language teaching and learning because some words are more useful to learn and use than others.

Effect of Context on Collocations

Looking beyond the effect of context on individual words, the interest of instructors can extend to words that tend to co-occur in writing with greater frequency than chance. To explain this, consider words that tend to appear with *coffee*. It would be much more likely to talk of *strong coffee* than *powerful coffee*, and thus *strong* and *coffee* are said to collocate. The term **collocations** describes these two-word lexical sequences. Researchers have investigated collocations in terms of two content words (*strong coffee*) and in terms of one content word and one function word (*give up*).

Durrant (2009) was interested in identifying both types of collocations that appear frequently across a range of academic subject areas as an exploratory study into the feasibility of developing a collocation list for academic purposes. Among the 1,000 collocations identified are these items sourced from the 100 most commonly occurring EAP collocations (Durrant, 2009: 166–168):

this study	*in addition*	*these findings*
due to	*determined by*	*over time*
consistent with	*correlated with*	*data set*
related to	*previous studies*	*shows that*
compared to	*control group*	*significant difference*

Some collocations on this list are combinations of content and function words (*related to, obtained from, defined as*) while other collocations are combinations of two content words (*control group, current study, sample size*). The use of such lists of collocations for pedagogical purposes will be shaped in part by teacher and student attitudes toward the use of collocations as well as student experiences with using collocations in their writing. The attraction for L2 students to use collocations could be to give their writing an expert or scholarly feel, although the effect on the reader will be shaped by the accuracy of use, the range of collocations used, and repetition of their use within the writing.

Lexical Bundles

Turning attention away from single words and collocations and toward larger sequences of words, the question arises whether we are still talking about vocabulary. When bundles of words behave similarly to single words in terms of the processes of learning and generating meaning, then these are best discussed from the perspective of vocabulary. To explain this idea further, a group of words that are learned and stored in memory as a unit are part of the mental lexicon. At what point does the **lexical bundle** become too long to be considered as a vocabulary item? A review of research studies suggests the focus is on lexical bundles of up to five or six words (see, e.g., Chen, 2019; Greaves & Warren, 2010; Hyland, 2008).

Figure 3.3: Academic Lexical Bundles

3-Word	4-Word	5-Word
in order to	*on the other hand*	*it should be noted that*
in terms of	*at the same time*	*it can be seen that*
as well as	*in the case of*	*due to the fact that*
the present study	*on the basis of*	*it can be observed that*
as a result	*it was found that*	*this may be due to*

Source: Hyland, 2008, p. 7. Used with permission of Elsevier.

One domain of language that has attracted particular attention for lexical bundles is academic writing. Hyland (2008) identified the most frequently occurring three-, four-, and five-word sequences in a 3.5 million-word corpus of articles, dissertations, and theses representing academic writing. Examples of these academic lexical bundles are shown in Figure 3.3.

These academic lexical bundles can be thought of as **formulaic language** in academic writing and could, in part, provide a useful framework for discussing ideas associated with scholarly research. As these are used by expert writers, L2 students may seek to acquire and use these bundles in their writing to provide their text with an expert or scholarly tone.

Use of Word Lists

Lists such as those discussed in this chapter describe vocabulary use in specific domains. They capture patterns of vocabulary use and identify the most significant words according to the criteria used. What are the implications of such lists for L2 writing? The answer to that question is complex. For some writing teachers, these lists will inform vocabulary teaching to prepare learners for the specific demands of subject-area study. For some L2 students, these lists will inform their independent vocabulary development.

The handling of academic words and technical words for students on an academic pathway may need to be different.

Technical words may best be acquired concurrently with learning the subject matter, on the assumption that these words are ideally viewed and learned in specific contexts and the expectation that the subject teacher will explain the technical words. However, this is not the case with academic words, suggesting a need to pre-teach these words in high school or pre-sessional (EAP) contexts.

Support programs can also play a useful role during an academic program of study where L2 learners studying nursing, for example, could have parallel classes that provide support with language aspects, including a direct focus on the vocabulary demands of writing nursing assignments reflective of the language of nursing.

Key Points

1. While some words are general purpose, in that they appear in a broad range of domains and contexts, other words have more restricted uses, reflected in more restricted domains. Among the latter are technical words that are subject-dependent and academic words that are subject-independent. Furthermore, some general service words can assume academic or technical meanings.
2. Specialist word lists need to build on a suitable core vocabulary. Thus, high school science word lists might build on K1 words, academic word lists suited to upper secondary students might build on K1 + K2 words, and graduate medicine word lists might build on K1 + K2 + AWL. The decision about what to consider as known or familiar words is central to the success of subsequent vocabulary learning.
3. The vocabulary learning needs of L2 students are shaped by their language proficiency, the type of writing they are completing now, and their future language situation. This means that a principled approach to vocabulary learning based on a needs analysis is a useful starting point for developing a vocabulary focus that exposes students to words they will need to use in their compositions.

Sample Activities for the Classroom

Activity 1: Elementary School Level

"Daily activities" is the focus of an L2 writing lesson with your elementary school students. You elicit from your students words that they know on the topic and ask them to write these on a large **graffiti board** in the classroom in the form of a large sheet of paper where students can write and draw (Flint, Dollar, & Stewart, 2018). Students then add drawings and related vocabulary items. The board becomes a focus for the ideas and language of daily activities, allowing students to become immersed in the subject-related language. The teacher models use of some of the words in sentences, such as:

- *I wake up at 7 AM.*
- *I have a shower before I go to bed.*

Students then construct a paragraph on the topic, writing about their daily activities. This topic-focused task helps students' development of vocabulary knowledge associated with a specific topic.

Activity 2: High School Level

Drawing on Nation and Gu (2007) regarding use of a textbook task originally appearing in Yeoh et al. (2002), Activity 2 presents a writing task designed for science students. This curriculum-based task for L2 settings encourages learners to interact with each other and the teacher to help learners clarify meanings and use vocabulary around a task designed to teach them that "objects with mass occupy space."

Steps

1. Students are given this information: "Matter is anything that has *mass* and *occupies space*. Water, air, and soil are examples of matter. They have mass and occupy space. Living things such as plants and animals are matter. They too have mass and occupy space."

2. The teacher asks the students to reflect on these questions:
   - What is mass?
   - Do water, soil, and air have mass, and do they occupy space?
3. The teacher reviews the meanings of these words that will be used in the activity: *record, weigh, total, attach, balance, observe, happens*. The teacher shares with students the sample sentences:
   - *Weigh an empty beaker and record its mass in grams.*
   - *Record the total mass of the beaker and soil.*
   - *Attach the balloons to the ends of a straw.*
   - *Balance the balloons by attaching cellophane tape.*
   - *Observe what happens to the balloons.*
4. The students complete these tasks in small groups:
   - Weigh an empty measuring cylinder and record its mass.
   - Half fill the cylinder with water and record the total mass.
   - Weigh an empty beaker and record its mass.
   - Half fill the beaker with soil and record the total mass.
   - Blow up two balloons.
   - Attach the balloons to each end of a straw and hang from the middle with string. Balance the balloons evenly by attaching cellophane tape to balloons as needed.
   - Using a pin, prick one balloon to release the air and observe what happens.
5. The students report on their findings to others to encourage productive use of the target language. The teacher asks them to explain what they understand about *mass* and *occupying space*.
6. In a later class, the teacher instructs the students to devise another small experiment related to mass and occupying space and to collaboratively write this up as a procedure. They are to do this without looking at the experiment just completed to encourage retrieval of target vocabulary items.
7. The teacher encourages students to share their written experiments with others in the class.

Activity 3: High School Level

Drawing on Nation and Gu (2007) regarding use of a textbook task originally appearing in Ash, Lofts, and Evergreen (1998: 28), Activity 3 displays a group-work activity for Grade 12 science students in a dual-language science classroom concerning "physical and chemical properties." Use of the L1 and L2 is encouraged to help activate prior knowledge with support from the bilingual teacher as required.

Steps

1. The teacher asks students working in small groups to discuss their answers to these questions:
   - What is meant by the term *physical property?*
   - What is meant by the term *chemical property?*
2. The teacher opens the discussion up at a class level to determine if students understand the terms well.
3. Working in small groups, students are asked to describe the physical properties of *ice, honey, gasoline, wool,* and *cement.*
4. The teacher then asks the students what chemical property is shared by *gasoline, wood, kerosene,* and *coal.*
5. The teacher asks the students to classify each of these properties as a physical or a chemical property in their small groups:
   odor, color, explosiveness, ability to warm when in the sun, solubility, smoothness, corrosiveness, lightness compared to air, colorlessness, susceptibility to rust, shininess, ability to float on water, being square shaped, tarnishing in air, producing bubbles when placed in acid
6. Any unclear vocabulary items in this list of properties are discussed as a class.
7. Students report their classifications to other groups in the class and attempt to clarify any unclear classifications.
8. The teacher asks the students to write a paragraph, with examples provided, that provides a description of the terms *physical property* and *chemical property.*

Activity 4: University Level

The L2 writing teacher in a university writing class is encouraging development of academic vocabulary in writing. A student has submitted an essay with this paragraph:

> COVID-19 was not the first world pandemic and will not be the last. In fact, some scientists are surprised that there have not been more world pandemics over the past 100 years, with gains in air travel. Our close world is weak to fast spread of infections, as we all have found out. In reality, humans will need to live with a variety of infections in the future, although attempts to make safe and workable vaccines will need to go on.

The teacher underlined words that could be substituted with words from the AWL and asked the student to consider alternative words that convey a more formal or scholarly tone in a subsequent draft. The student then submitted this revision and sought feedback on the revisions. This process shifts the student toward use of a more academic register:

> COVID-19 was not the first global pandemic and will not be the last. In fact, some scientists are surprised that there have not been more global pandemics over the past 100 years, with improvements in air travel. Our interconnected world is prone to rapid spread of infections, as we all have discovered. In reality, humans will need to live with a range of infections in the future, although attempts to develop safe and effective vaccines will need to continue.

Tasks and Discussion Questions for Teachers

1. L2 students at a secondary school are facing difficulty understanding some of the technical language in science textbooks. This includes words such as *method, data, analyze, predict, hypothesis, measure,* which they are not familiar with from their previous language studies. Teachers have seen students writing L1 translations in their science textbooks as annotations, with some students spending most of the class time on this, meaning they are not spending adequate time on set tasks in class. What do you feel the teacher could do to assist these students?
2. In an advanced EAP program, you want students to use newly acquired academic words in writing tasks that reflect the types of writing they will undertake at university. You feel that the current syllabus focuses on text types (e.g., argumentative, compare/contrast) that might not fully reflect the way words are used in academic settings. How might you approach this issue?
3. You have been contracted to prepare and deliver a 12-week course for a group of 16 government officials from Peru and have been advised that they all have an intermediate proficiency in English and are from a range of government departments including foreign ministry, commerce, and social services. How might you approach the vocabulary component for this program? What considerations would inform this process?

Chapter 4

Measuring Vocabulary Use in Writing

GUIDING QUESTIONS

1. What is known about the vocabulary size of L2 writers?
2. How does vocabulary use affect the quality of L2 writing?
3. How can teachers measure vocabulary use in writing?

This chapter discusses general approaches to measuring vocabulary size and knowledge before addressing specific approaches to measure vocabulary use in relation to writing. Attention is given to the concepts of lexical diversity and lexical sophistication, with discussion of how these characteristics shape writing quality. Examples of student writing inform the discussion.

Why Measure Vocabulary Size and Knowledge?

Students develop lexical quality in their writing over time because of students' exposure to the language, opportunities to produce writing, and feedback on vocabulary use in their writing. As the lexicon of a student develops, the lexical quality of the student's writing improves. Thus, it would be natural to expect that instructors can capture a picture of a student's developing lexicon through the words used in writing. Some of the interest in measuring the lexical quality of writing is as a means to measure the vocabulary knowledge of the writer, which then leads to an interest in the type of writing being assessed and the tools used to measure vocabulary use.

Approaches to Measuring Vocabulary

There is a strong focus in L2 vocabulary research on measuring vocabulary size and knowledge in a general sense. For example, to capture the vocabulary size of different cohorts of language users, Nation (1983) developed a **Vocabulary Levels Test** to measure receptive knowledge of vocabulary at levels of 2,000, 3,000, 5,000, 10,000, and university words, illustrated in the test item shown in Figure 4.1 where students match words on the left with meanings on the right.

Subsequent development of a **Controlled Productive Vocabulary Levels Test** (Laufer & Nation, 1999: 48) was intended to measure knowledge of words that could be used productively at the same five levels (2,000, 3,000, 5,000, 10,000, and university words) in a controlled sentence format, as shown:

The urge to survive is inh________ in all creatures.

Figure 4.1: Test Item from Vocabulary Levels Test

1. alter	____ change
2. coincide	____ say something is not true
3. deny	____ describe clearly and exactly
4. devote	
5. release	
6. specify	

Source: Schmitt, Schmitt, & Clapham, 2001, p 85. Used with permission of Sage.

These test formats can be used to report the **receptive** (i.e., the ability to match a word form with a meaning) and **controlled productive** (i.e., the ability to complete a missing word in a sentence) vocabulary sizes of different groups of learners. Both formats are designed to report on vocabulary size through a sampling method.

Meara and Alcoy (2010) reflect on the limitations of these approaches to measure the vocabulary knowledge of learners because the test formats use a **sampling** method to make wider assumptions about the learner's lexicon, in much the same way as someone might make assumptions about the number of fish in a river system by sampling a small section of the river. The challenge in measuring productive vocabulary size is to provide learners with a writing prompt that taps into learners' full lexicon and then to measure this word use. As this is unrealistic, researchers rely on estimates.

Moving away from measures of vocabulary size to now reflect on vocabulary knowledge in the depth dimension, Read (1993, 1998) developed a **Word Associates Test (WAT)** to measure depth-of-word knowledge in terms of **paradigmatic** (in the form of synonyms) and **syntagmatic** (in the form of collocations) components, as in this example (Read, 1998: 46):

sudden
beautiful quick surprising thirsty //
change doctor noise school

Matching the test-item word *sudden* with *quick* and *surprising* would suggest knowledge of synonyms, while matching *sudden* with *change* and *noise* would suggest knowledge of collocations. The test format provides a means to explore a learner's mental lexicon as a representation of the depth dimension of vocabulary knowledge.

To capture distinctions in knowledge of words along the partial-precise continuum, Wesche and Paribakht (1996) devised a **Vocabulary Knowledge Scale (VKS)** where students

Figure 4.2: Vocabulary Knowledge Scale

I. I don't remember having seen this word before.

II. I have seen this word before, but I don't know what it means.

III. I have seen this word before, and I think it means ________. (synonym or translation)

IV. I know this word. It means ________. (synonym or translation)

V. I can use this word in a sentence: ________. (Write a sentence) (If you do this section, please also do Section IV.)

Source: Paribakht & Wesche, 1997, p. 180. Used with permission of Cambridge University Press.

self-report their level of word knowledge using descriptors and prompts. Figure 4.2 shows the five levels of knowledge in the VKS.

Beyond Level V of the VKS, it would be expected to see knowledge continue to develop as new forms and meanings of the word are added to a student's lexicon, and as the associations between the target word and other known words develop as new understandings of the world and new experiences affect the way words are seen to relate to each other.

Measuring Vocabulary Use in L2 Writing

Aside from these assessment instruments, vocabulary assessment has played a role in the holistic assessment of L2 writing. Yoon (2018), for example, presents an assessment framework including descriptors for content, organization, vocabulary, language use, and mechanics, with vocabulary descriptors covering four distinct levels of writing (see Figure 4.3).

With more direct measurement of the lexical component of writing, approaches to measuring vocabulary use in writing have tended to explore two dimensions of lexical richness: lexical diversity and lexical sophistication.

Figure 4.3: Vocabulary Descriptors

Scoring (out of 20)	Vocabulary Descriptors
16–20	• Very sophisticated vocabulary • Excellent choice of words with no errors • Excellent range of vocabulary • Idiomatic and near native-like vocabulary • Academic register
11–15	• Somewhat sophisticated vocabulary. Attempts, even if not completely successful, at sophisticated vocabulary • Good choice of words with some errors that don't obscure meaning • Adequate range of vocabulary but some repetition • Approaching academic register
6–10	• Unsophisticated vocabulary • Limited word choice with some errors obscuring meaning • Repetitive choice of words • No resemblance to academic register
0–5	• Very simple vocabulary • Severe errors in word choice that often obscure meaning • No variety in word choice • No resemblance to academic register

Source: Adapted from Yoon, 2018, p. 402. Used with permission of Taylor & Francis.

Lexical Diversity

As a way to consider approaches to measuring vocabulary use in writing, Figure 4.4 shows an L2 high school student response to the prompt "How earthquakes occur."

Figure 4.4: Student Text on "How Earthquakes Occur"

How Earthquakes Occur

Write a paragraph of around 250 words using the following terms (you can change word form as needed): *tectonic plates, molten lava, continental shift, movement, collisions, shock waves, frequent, prediction.*

Everybody has heard of earthquakes. In my country, we sometimes have earthquakes but not so many. They are like unknown things that suddenly arrive. Most people including my family are very afraid of them, and I am too. They can happen any time like at night and day or on weekends and school days. Why do we have earthquakes? The world is round and has continents under the ground. They are called tectonic plates. Every continent is like a home, but not still. They sometimes move left or right. Under the earth is molten lava, so continents can move easily like fluid. That is called continental shift. Especially countries like Japan and Indonesia have this. When they collide there is shaking and sometimes noise too. That is earthquakes happening. Earthquakes have shock waves moving in all directions. It is like explosions when earthquakes happen. If we live in the middle of continent, we have less earthquakes because the land is not colliding. That is why some countries have frequent earthquakes and some don't. My grandmother can predict earthquakes but only sometimes. She has a special feeling, like birds and animals that fly away all the time when an earthquake comes. Last month my grandmother rang my mother. I was so worried. But there was no earthquake. Maybe earthquakes send a warning like a sound or movement in the ground. I hope in the future scientists can predict them and give us a warning. Then we can live in a secure and safe world and not have dangerous accidents happen from shaking and houses falling over.

Source: Based on an anonymous unpublished student text used with permission.

The text has 266 running words (or individual word occurrences), also known as **tokens**. The text makes use of 139 different words or **types**. In the text, some words are repeated, such as *have* (ten times), *like* (eight times), *the* (eight times), *we* (six times), and *when* (three times). The relationship between tokens and types in this text provides an indication of **lexical diversity** (i.e., the range of different words used) by calculating the **type-token ratio (TTR)**. For this text, the TTR = 0.54, a measurement of the extent of word repetition. The idea is that greater lexical diversity corresponds with a larger vocabulary size, on the assumption that students with larger vocabulary sizes are less inclined to repeat words. A text with no repetitions would have a lexical diversity score of 1.0, while a text with 50 percent repetitions (i.e., an average of two repetitions per type) would receive a lexical diversity score of 0.5. Thus, the higher the value (i.e., closer to 1.0), the greater the lexical diversity. If new words were introduced into the above text in place of repetitions, the lexical diversity measure increases.

One of the concerns with TTR as a measure of overall lexical richness, as discussed in Durán et al. (2004), is that the ratio can be affected by text length such that comparisons continue to be made across the text as text length increases, which in turn increases the prospects for word repetition. A common thought might be that shorter texts may have an advantage over longer texts, but this is an overly simplistic view. However, to explain this concern, consider the three texts shown in Figure 4.5.

Figure 4.5: TTR Comparison of Three Texts

Text	TTR Value
Whether to live in the countryside or city is not a big issue.	1.00 (13 tokens : 13 types)
As far as I am concerned, whether to live in the countryside or city is not a big issue.	0.95 (19 tokens : 18 types)
As far as I am concerned, whether to live in the countryside or city is not a big issue because I am happy to live anywhere if I have my family.	0.81 (31 tokens : 25 types)

The shortest text avoids repetition and thus has the highest lexical diversity possible of 1.00. The second text has a lower lexical diversity score of 0.95, affected by the repetition of the word *as*. The third text introduces even more repetition of words, resulting in the lowest lexical diversity value of 0.81. Once low-proficiency students have exhausted known vocabulary, they tend to increase repetition of words as text length increases. Thus, particularly for learners with small vocabulary sizes, controlling text length when measuring TTR is important.

Malvern and Richards (2002) propose an alternative measure of TTR, termed D, designed to address the concern that simple ratio TTR values tend to decline as text length increases. D allows for more meaningful comparisons of lexical diversity of texts of varying length. Another approach is that proposed by McCarthy and Jarvis (2010) in the form of a measure of textual lexical diversity (MTLD), similarly addressing concerns with the simple TTR calculations.

With TTR, no direct account is taken of whether words used are commonplace or rare, which moves our attention to another measure of vocabulary use in writing—lexical sophistication.

Lexical Sophistication

Researchers employ a measure of **lexical sophistication** to provide a picture of the types of words used in writing, in terms of more and less commonly used. To distinguish between words used, Laufer and Nation (1995) group them according to existing word lists such as K1 (first 1,000), K2 (second 1,000), AWL (academic words), and other words (which could include proper nouns, technical words, and lower-frequency words), otherwise known as a **lexical frequency profile (LPF)**. These word lists reflect the natural word acquisition order, starting with the highest-frequency general service words, then academic words, and then lower-frequency words. The LFP for the earthquake paragraph in Figure 4.4 is shown in Figure 4.6.

Figure 4.6: Lexical Profile of the Earthquake Text

Word List	Percentage of Tokens (%)	Example Word Families
K1	88.39	*a, all, and, animal, any, arrive, away, be, because, bird, but, call, can, come, country, danger, day, direct, do, earth, easy, every, fall, family, feel, fly, from, future, give, ground, happen, have, hear, home, hope, house, I, if, in, include, it, know, last, left, less, like, live, make, many, maybe, middle, month, most, mother, move, night, no, not, of, on, only, or, over, people, right, ring, round, safe, school, science, send, shake, she, so, some, sound, special, still, the, then, there, they, thing, this, time, too, under, very, wave, we, week, when, why, world*
K2	5.24	*accident, afraid, especial, explode, frequent, grand, noise, plate, shock, sudden, warn, worry*
AWL	1.50	*predict, secure, shift*
Other words	4.87	*collide, continent, fluid, Indonesia, Japan, lava, molten, tectonic*
Total	100.00	

An alternative approach to lexical profiling of higher-level or sophisticated writing is to identify words and corresponding percentages for groups of 1,000 words represented as K1, K2, K3, K4, K5, and up to K10 based on the BNC and the COCA lists. These word lists can be referred to as BNC/COCA 1–10. In this approach, there is no separate identification of academic words. The academic words are embedded within the BNC/COCA lists, as exemplified in Figure 4.7.

Figure 4.7: Embedding of Academic Words within the BNC/COCA Word Lists

BNC/COCA List	Number of Academic Words	Examples of Academic Words
1	283	*access, consume, data, involve, voluntary*
2	63	*assist, benefit, investigate, survive, vehicle*
3	161	*abandon, confirm, exhibit, philosophy, virtual*
4	48	*ambiguous, hierarchy, integral, preliminary, unify*
5	11	*albeit, deviate, intrinsic, paradigm, qualitative*
6	3	*discrete, finite, notwithstanding*
7	1	*ethic*
8	0	
9	0	
10	0	

The BNC/COCA lists provide a detailed picture of vocabulary use across a broad range of frequency levels, as shown in the vocabulary analysis of the earthquakes text (in Figure 4.4) in Figure 4.8.

The choice of word lists used in an analysis of vocabulary use in writing should reflect the learning context. Consider a paragraph, shown in Figure 4.9, written by an L2 primary school student on the topic of "My family."

Figure 4.8: Lexical Profile of Text Based on BNC/COCA 1–10

BNC/COCA Word List	Percentage of Tokens (%)	Example Word Families
1	85.4	*a, afraid, all, and, animal, any, arrive, away, be, because, bird, but, call, can, come, country, danger, day, do, easy, especially, every, fall, family, feel, fly, from, give, grandfather, ground, happen, have, hear, home, hope, house, I, if, in, it, know, last, left, less, like, live, make, many, maybe, middle, month, most, mother, move, night, no, noise, not, of, on, only, or, over, people, right, ring, round, safe, school, science, secure, send, shake, she, so, some, sound, special, still, sudden, that, the, then, there, they, thing, time, too, under, very, wave, we, when, why, world, worry*
2	3.4	*accident, direction, future, include, plate, shift, shock, warn*
3	3.4	*continent, explosion, frequent, predict*
4	0.4	*fluid*
5	4.5	*earthquake*
6	1.1	*collide*
7	0	
8	0.4	*molten*
9	0.4	*tectonic*
10	0	
Other words	0	
Total	100.00	

Figure 4.9: Student Text on "My Family"

My Family

I live with my nuclear family. In my family, I have my mother, my father, my older brother and my older sister. I am the youngest child. We also have a pet dog. His name is Snowball and he is very active. We built a special house for him outside in the garden. We were given him by our neighbours when they shifted house. In my home there are many rooms, so I have my own bedroom. My parents are both teachers, and my siblings already go to high school. I will commence high school too when I turn 13. Sometimes my paternal grandparents visit us. When they come I share a room with my sister. That is always exciting.

Source: Based on an anonymous unpublished student text used with permission.

For young writers or low-level students, it might be useful to discriminate within high-frequency vocabulary to capture development within the first 2,000 words of English. This could be in 250-word segments, starting with the most frequently occurring 250 words, and then continuing. These lists can be called Kids 250–01, Kids 250–02, Kids 250–03, and up through to Kids 250–10. The VocabProfile for the text in Figure 4.9 based on the Kids-250 word lists appears in Figure 4.10.

Meara and Bell (2001) proposed an alternative measure of lexical sophistication, P-Lex, which would be suitable for young or low-level learners who produce short texts. They explain that the LFP is not designed to work well with short texts and show that by examining word choice within ten-word segments, P-Lex calculates a score that is not directly affected by text length. P-Lex compares words from the K1 word list with other words it classifies as "difficult." This calculation provides a P-Lex profile.

Aside from the preceding measures of vocabulary use in writing, researchers have been interested in the effect of the writing prompt on the activation of word knowledge in writing. This is based on the idea that some idea fields will be more lexically developed for a group of L2 writers than others based on previous instructional exposure and life experiences. Akbarian, Farajollahi, and Catalán (2020) found that their EFL

Figure 4.10: Lexical Profile of Text Based on Kids-250 Word Lists

Kids-250 Word List	Percentage of Tokens (%)	Vocabulary Items
01	73.73	*a, always, and, be, bed, brother, by, come, dog, for, give, go, grand, have, he, home, house, I, in, live, mother, name, old, out, room, sister, so, some, the, there, they, this, to, too, we, when, will, with*
02	7.63	*already, both, build, father, many, own, teach, very*
03	4.24	*also, family, pet, special*
04	3.39	*child, neighbor, share, visit*
05	0.85	*excite*
06	1.69	*garden, snowball*
07	0.00	
08	0.85	*parent*
09	0.00	
10	2.54	*high school, young*
Other words	5.08	*active, commence, nuclear, paternal, shift, sibling*
Total	100.00	

learners exhibited a greater number of word types for topics related to parts of the body, animals, and school compared to countryside and means of transportation. They hypothesized that the former topics were introduced earlier in the language learning process, and thus were associated with more well-developed lexical knowledge than the latter topics.

This issue reflects a broader research interest in the effect of writing task prompts on student performance and use of strategies (Shi, Huang, & Lu, 2020) with the finding that "prompt type significantly affected the participants' overall continuation writing scores, syntactic complexity, cohesion, and source-use features. It also significantly affected the participants' monitoring strategy" (p. 361). This is particularly significant when writing tasks are used to report on test-taker language knowledge in high-stakes contexts, such as for university admission and migration purposes.

Measuring Use of Collocations and Lexical Bundles

While there are well-developed tools to measure single word use in writing, measuring collocation and lexical chunk use in writing has not attracted the same attention for different reasons. One reason for this is that a computer analysis tool would view any two words co-occurring in writing as a collocation. Beyond two words, identifying meaningful items becomes even more problematic in terms of identifying acceptable forms of lexical bundles. Thus, *on a* may be wrongly counted as a collocation and *is an easy* as a lexical bundle.

Researchers have used a multistep approach to overcome this issue. Laufer and Waldman (2011) were interested in identifying noun-verb collocations appearing in student writing. The methodology they adopted enabled identification of collocations:

- Create a corpus of the student writing to be analyzed.
- Using the WordSmith Tools software package, scan the corpus for nouns, and list these by decreasing frequency.
- Depending on the corpus size, set a cut-off frequency to identify the most frequently occurring nouns.
- Using WordSmith Tools functions, identify verb-noun collocations for these frequently occurring nouns.
- Check the resulting list of potential collocations against the BBI Dictionary of English Word Combinations (Benson, Benson, & Ilson, 1997) and the LTP Dictionary of Selected Collocations (Hill & Morgan, 1997) to identify those regarded as collocations.

While this is a time-consuming and involved process, it generates useful data on student use of collocations that can inform a language learning program.

Teacher Judgments of Lexical Quality in Writing

Researchers have tended to investigate the role of vocabulary in teacher judgments of writing by comparing aspects of vocabulary in writing at different proficiency levels based on human and computerized rating systems.

Grant and Ginther (2000) compared use of vocabulary, including lexical diversity (type/token ratio) and average word length, in L2 writing at three proficiency levels. They found that, as proficiency level increased as rated using a rating scale, L2 writers incorporated more unique words in their essays and that average word length also increased.

Guo, Crossley, and McNamara (2013) found that linguistic features including lexical sophistication, syntactic complexity, cohesion, and basic text information were significant predictors of L2 writing proficiency.

Vögelin et al. (2019) explored the relations between lexical diversity and lexical sophistication on teachers' judgments of ESL argumentative essays, finding that "texts with greater lexical diversity and sophistication were assessed more positively concerning their overall quality" (p. 50).

The overall picture gained from such studies is that lexical diversity and lexical sophistication affect judgments of writing proficiency and thus are an important means of assessing the quality of written compositions.

Computer programs increasingly used in such analysis include **Coh-Metrix** (Graesser et al., 2004) and **TAALES (Tool for the Automatic Analysis of Lexical Sophistication)** (Kyle, Crossley, & Berger, 2018), which allow researchers to explore a broad range of features of language use.

Key Points

1. In the context of L2 writing, a key focus of measuring vocabulary is to provide a profile of the types of words students use. This can shape future learning to help students acquire and use the words they need.
2. Lexical diversity and lexical sophistication are widely used to evaluate word use in writing.
3. Teachers and students can use online tools that provide a vocabulary profile of writing. This would indicate words used according to pre-determined word lists such as K1, K2, and the AWL, with tailoring of word lists to suit the context of learning and the language proficiency of the learners.

Tasks and Discussion Questions for Teachers

1. It is common in some large language programs to pre-test student vocabulary knowledge to place them into suitable language classes based on levels such as beginners, intermediate, and advanced. But this is not always possible, particularly in school settings where L2 students may be integrated into mainstream classrooms for subjects such as science and history. Do you feel that students with wide-ranging vocabulary sizes can be given similar writing tasks? What might be some issues arising from this?
2. "Vocabulary profiles provide a limited picture of overall word use in writing." To what extent do you agree with this statement, and what do the vocabulary profiles not tell us?
3. Topic choice affects students' use of words and text length. How could you set up a task to capture your students' richest use of words?

Chapter 5

Encouraging and Improving Productive Use of Words

GUIDING QUESTIONS

1. How can L2 students be encouraged to use a wider range of words in their writing?
2. What is the relative value of indirect and direct approaches to vocabulary teaching for improving the lexical component of L2 student writing?
3. Is productive use of words enhanced more by the quantity or quality of exposure to words?

This chapter explores different approaches to encourage and improve use of vocabulary in the writing of L2 students. The discussion begins by considering the relationship between receptive and productive words and how the activation of words in writing is shaped by dimensions of word knowledge. This leads to a discussion about incidental and direct approaches to teaching, presenting a model of implicit and explicit word processing as a continuum. The focus then moves to the reading-writing connection and the provision of a thematic link between reading material and writing tasks. The chapter documents the conditions that appear to favor vocabulary learning in a general sense, with implications for the L2 writing teacher. It then considers approaches to providing feedback on vocabulary use in writing, with sensitivity to the social setting of the writing. An overview draws together the main ideas of the chapter with considerations to classroom practice.

How Words Are Acquired for Productive Use

Some words that are known receptively are not evident in productive use. We know this because measures of L2 vocabulary knowledge in participant groups indicate receptive vocabulary sizes larger than productive vocabulary sizes (Laufer, 1998; Zhong, 2018). Laufer's (1998) data, for example, show that, although receptive vocabulary sizes continue to advance well beyond the 2,000-word list, sometimes what occurs is a "plateauing out" of word use in the productive realm, exhibited by an overdependence on more familiar words at the expense of less common words. This has implications for bilingual and dual language immersion programs where L2 writers aspire to achieve native-like command of their writing, as discussed in de Jong (2004):

> the analysis indicated a possible "plateau" effect for productive language skills. This finding has important implications for ELL programs. Long-term persistence of an intermediate plateau may eventually prevent ELLs from having full access to academically complex learning environments that make more sophisticated demands on their language skills. Teachers must therefore learn to pay conscious attention to academic English proficiency, especially after initial fluency has been reached. (p. 104)

Part of the issue may be a lack of incentives to utilize less common or more precise words in writing, resulting in students avoiding words that they do not feel confident manipulating (Xu & Wu, 2012); this then suggests a tendency for L2 writers to take the more well-trodden path that is perceived to be safer. Of course, this is dependent to an extent on the personality traits of individual L2 writers and on the fact that some words encountered while reading or listening may not be useful or appropriate in writing. Another part of the issue may be what Coxhead and Byrd (2007) have portrayed as vocabulary's closer association with reading than with writing, as in this case in the context of EAP programs:

> The tradition in ESL/EFL has been to make vocabulary learning the responsibility of the "reading teacher" with the result that vocabulary is often approached at the recognition level rather than with the ultimate goal of having the students learn to use the academic words in their own writing. (p. 133)

Folse (2010) provides further insights into the significance attached to vocabulary in the language classroom, suggesting that the variance reported among teachers in their approach to vocabulary instruction reflects differing teacher practices that have been shaped by their understandings, values, and experiences learning vocabulary. It would appear, then, that teachers can be trained to enhance the significance attached to teaching vocabulary in the L2 classroom.

For L2 writing teachers, understanding the process of acquiring and activating receptive vocabulary knowledge is helpful when encouraging L2 students to use a wider lexicon in their writing. This brings us to the relationship between **receptive** word knowledge, largely developed through exposure to comprehensible spoken and written language, and **productive** word knowledge, as a means to understand the process of activating known words in writing. To help us understand the receptive-productive vocabulary relationship, Henriksen (1999) presents a model of L2 vocabulary knowledge in which words enter the lexicon receptively and then may become available for productive use. The process of transfer of words from receptive to productive use is shaped by the quality of the word knowledge, including understandings of different forms and meanings of the word, synonyms, associations, and collocations. To illustrate this, as students develop understandings of the word *mammal* in a school setting through reading and classroom learning activities, they will become more confident in using the word in their writing in an increasing range of contexts. Student knowledge of different aspects of word knowledge typically occurs incrementally, progressing along a continuum from **partial** to **precise** (see Chapter 1) and reflecting distinct levels or degrees of understanding. This model of vocabulary learning assumes a threshold at which receptive vocabulary knowledge is transformed into productive vocabulary knowledge, shaped by **depth** and **precision** of word knowledge (Henriksen & Haastrup, 1998). On this point, mastery of the word *mammal* would require a greater depth of understanding and precision of use than would apply to *cat* or *dog*, given that *mammal* is conceptually complex. Thus, the threshold for activation of vocabulary in writing varies from word to word.

Incidental and Direct Vocabulary Learning

In debates about whether students acquire vocabulary best as a process of **implicit learning**—that is, when the focus is on ideas rather than on individual vocabulary items—or as a process of **explicit learning**, with conscious attention given to the occurrence of words in the language, these two points should be considered:

- Implicit-explicit learning might best be conceived of as a continuum, rather than mutually exclusive alternatives, suggesting that both processes can occur at the same time.
- Labeling a task or activity as promoting implicit learning or explicit learning of vocabulary does not necessarily extend to the processes engaged by the learner.

Thus, it's all too easy to make assumptions, based on task design, on the way in which vocabulary learning is operating, but, as Schmidt (1994) reminds us, "learning takes place only within the learner" (p. 21) and may be independent of the activity goal or design.

One possible starting point for discussing how words are made available for productive use is to explore the development of vocabulary knowledge because that process has implications for whether words will be transferred into writing. However, the theoretical understanding of this process is sketchy, as Meara (1998) has observed:

> Theoretical books on vocabulary acquisition have more problems than most .... The main difficulty, as I see it, is that we just do not have a comprehensive theory of vocabulary acquisition which could be exploited to produce practical advice for how vocabulary should be taught. We have some handy rules of thumb about what a reasonable vocabulary load is, and there is a general agreement over what kinds of exercises are effective, but that is about as far as it goes. (p. 290)

While there is no comprehensive model of how words are acquired and made available for productive use, there is research and pedagogical interest in both incidental and direct approaches to vocabulary development given the fact that teachers value a repertoire of approaches for promoting the lexical component of their student's writing. Let's look first at incidental approaches.

Extensive reading, as a means of providing students with large quantities of comprehensible input where the focus is on meaning, has attracted considerable research attention in terms of its potential contribution to vocabulary development. This reflects broader interest within SLA theory of the role of **comprehensible input** in language development (Krashen, 1989). There is empirical evidence in ESL contexts for the value of extensive reading in L2 writing development in a general sense, in which extensive reading material is introduced into the L2 classroom with a central pedagogical interest in utilizing the reading material. Elley's (2000) report of **book flood** studies in rural primary schools in Niue, Fiji, the Solomon Islands, Sri Lanka, Singapore, and South Africa indicated more improvements in writing skill for students in classrooms using the book flood approach when compared to children in schools with a traditional focus on textbooks as the sole source of reading materials. Key factors here are selecting suitable reading materials in terms of language and content and ensuring a central role for extensive reading both in and outside the language classroom. Graded readers have been developed specifically for this purpose because vocabulary is controlled at proficiency levels and indicates the number of word families used (i.e., 200, 300, 600, 1,200, 1,700, 2,300, 3,000). Additionally, grammatical structures, sentence length and complexity, number of words per page, and overall length of the book are also controlled. Beyond the 3,000-word level, a broader range of reading material can be accessed, with specific relevance to the language needs of the L2 students.

Of more direct significance to the focus of teaching vocabulary in writing, Horst, Cobb, and Meara's (1998) study with EFL students looked at the effect of reading on vocabulary acquisition. In their study, 34 intensive English students in Oman read along to a simplified version of the *Mayor of Casterbridge* as the teacher read the novel aloud in class in sections over a ten-day period. Aside from this, the students had no other exposure to the novel during the experimental period and there was minimal opportunity for intentional focus on new words as the teacher read the book aloud. The study therefore provided a controlled extensive listening-reading experience with the focus on pleasurable engagement with the novel. Researchers identified 23 words outside the K1 (first 1,000) and K2 (second 1,000) word lists, including words appearing between 2 to 17 times in the text. Students were then tested before and after on receptive knowledge of these words, indicating that they were unknown to the participants. Thus, the researchers sought a controlled focus on the effect of number of word meetings during the listening-reading experience on vocabulary learning. The findings indicated that the participants learned, on average, 5 of 23 unknown words, which represents just over 20 percent of the unknown words that appear more than once in the text. In addition, students were likely to learn unknown words occurring eight or more times in the text. Learning was less predictable below this threshold.

These findings suggest that some words appearing frequently in extensive reading material can be acquired incidentally when met. In addition, there is an ideal window for acquiring new words while reading (see Figure 5.1). If students know too few words, there is inadequate context for incidental vocabulary learning to occur, and if they know all the words in a text, there is no opportunity for acquiring new words (Nation, 2001).

Horst, Cobb, and Meara's (1998) study did not examine the effect of new meetings of previously known words in terms of enhancing depth and precision of word knowledge, although this type of consolidation of word knowledge is a key attraction of extensive reading programs as a means to prepare word knowledge for activation in writing. Overall, extensive reading is seen as an important means of adding new words to the lexicon, albeit in a slow way, and of consolidating word knowledge, thereby building up the lexicon for use in writing.

Figure 5.1: The Lexical Window for Learning Words in Context

The Lexical Window

Ask students to highlight all the unknown words in a sample of text they are reading and calculate the percentage of known words as a measure of lexical coverage. For a 100-word sample, this would be as follows:

- 2 unknown words = 98% familiarity
- 5 unknown words = 95% familiarity
- 10 unknown words = 90% familiarity

We then use the following as a guide, representing three thresholds for lexical coverage of known words:

- 90%: Students require assistance with learning new words in context (such as through use of glossaries, dictionaries, and teacher translations).
- 95–98%: Ideal window for learning new words from texts, where use of contextual clues can assist vocabulary learning.
- 100%: No opportunity to learn new words, but there is an opportunity to deepen knowledge of previously met words.

Given the relatively slow process of adding new words incidentally through extensive reading, let us focus on enhancing vocabulary learning opportunities while reading to speed up and improve vocabulary acquisition as a lexical resource for writing. This involves a more direct approach to vocabulary learning than is the case with extensive reading programs and can be applied particularly with short reading texts. Barcroft (2015) suggests two approaches to combining reading activities with an explicit focus on learning new words:

- **input-based effects,** in which target words are presented in texts with glossing or textual enhancement such as bold font or underlining to increase the odds of learners noticing the target words.
- **task-based effects** that require learners to perform different types of semantic tasks, such as answering questions about word meaning, and controlled writing tasks, to promote engagement with target words.

Figure 5.2 illustrates the applications of input-based and task-based effects in the sample tasks shown.

Textual enhancement (bolding, etc.), as an input-based effect, has attracted research attention because of its importance in facilitating **noticing of words**, which is an important

Figure 5.2: Input-Based and Task-Based Effects

Approach	Sample Types
Input-based effects	• *Textual enhancement*: underlining, boldfacing, italicizing, or capitalizing target words in the text to promote noticing • *Input enrichment*: seeding input with extra examples of the target item to increase meetings with the item
Task-based effects	• *Explicit instruction*: activities providing direct instruction of target words, covering word form, meaning, and use • *Meaningful output*: controlled sentence writing tasks with target words

Source: Summarized from Rassaei, 2012, pp. 6–8.

starting point for learning engagement (Schmidt, 1990). When students are drawn to target words through boldface or underlining, for example, they spend more time processing the items than would otherwise occur (Cho, 2017), which provides an important step in the process of acquiring words—namely, using them. Similarly, enriching input by providing multiple opportunities to meet target words through a modified text, as another input-based effect, can increase students' exposure to important words (Rassaei, 2012). A combination of input enrichment (increasing the number of meetings of target words) and textual enhancement (promoting noticing of target words) could be applied.

Researchers have also been interested in task-based effects, where the attention is on learner engagement with target words appearing in the text. Wang (2015), for example, reported on the use of teacher instruction on word meaning and use, gap-fill tasks requiring use of a target word in context, and comprehension tasks focusing on the meaning of target words as means to encourage uptake of words while reading. Ma and Choen (2018), in another example, presented the use of an English-Korean bilingual dictionary on a smartphone with Grade 10 EFL students in a Korean high school to engage students with target words while reading expository texts on global issues. These items were: *destructive, dramatically, worsen, preventable, conflict, up-to-date, afford, operator, correspondence, course, plantation, deforestation, ecology, coral, reef, amphibian, endanger, mass, substance,* and *ultraviolet.* Both these studies showed significant engagement in vocabulary learning during the experimental period. Such task-based effects provide a focus on words seen as central to the students' learning program.

In weighing the relative value of incidental and direct approaches to vocabulary development with a goal of improving students' word usage in their writing, it is important to note that empirical studies with participant groups have not given a clear picture of the best or preferred approach to vocabulary development (Shirzad, Rasekh, & Dabaghi, 2017). As a result, it is difficult to manipulate the internal process of word learning through task design in a measurable way. What studies have suggested, when viewed collectively, is that the process of acquiring words is complex and multifaceted and that a range of approaches, both incidental and more direct, can be useful to allow students to develop sufficient knowledge of words to use them confidently in writing.

The Reading-Writing Connection

Much of the writing undertaken in the L2 classroom has as its starting point reading (Hirvela, 2016), so the link between reading and writing is worth exploring in more detail through a vocabulary perspective. Teachers can provide a link between reading and writing through topic alignment, where the reading and writing tasks are thematically linked, and through identification of target vocabulary, where teachers emphasize key words during close reading. This link creates a better opportunity for increased uptake of useful words by students from these reading-into-writing tasks.

Lee (2003) adopted the idea of thematically linking reading and writing with ESL high school students in Canada to increase the productive use of target words appearing in a reading text. Lee added vocabulary instruction to the reading activity to provide both ideas and vocabulary support for a subsequent writing task. A key feature of the approach was that the target vocabulary appeared in the reading text with rich contextual significance for the subsequent writing task. The study showed a significant increase in the use of target vocabulary in the writing task associated with the approach adopted. The reading-to-writing approach has also been promoted by Coxhead (2006), who emphasizes its importance in the context of academic writing tasks like essays and reports, where the process of reading and researching a topic provides students with exposure to both technical and academic vocabulary, as well as in the context of overall ideas development. Engineering students preparing to write on the topic of "hydrogen fuel cells" can be instructed to read texts on the topic and identify words that would be use-

Figure 5.3: Controlled Writing Task

Controlled Writing Task

Write a paragraph on one of the following topics using five of the words listed. You may need to change the part of speech of the words you are using.

Social Media	or	**Inventions**	
technology	*community*	*conflict*	*evolve*
transform	*affect*	*social*	*economic*
invention	*modernization*	*develop*	*household*

Source: Adapted from Coxhead, 2006, p. 128. Used with permission of Cengage Learning.

ful to describe technical ideas (i.e., technical terminology), as well as terms that would bring a strong academic or scholarly tone and precision to their writing (i.e., academic vocabulary). Students could be encouraged to share their vocabulary learning process with other students as a collective learning activity. In this way, the reading-writing connection assumes a strong lexical dimension. This process is particularly relevant to academic writing tasks, where students are generally expected to include target vocabulary they encountered in their reading. This could be promoted through controlled paragraph writing tasks in which students are prompted to activate words already studied in class (see Figure 5.3).

The use of a controlled writing task is designed to serve as a stepping-stone to facilitate use of target words in subsequent writing, based on the assumption that students will recognize the semantic value of these words in writing while gaining experience and confidence in using them productively.

Conditions Favoring Vocabulary Learning

For students to use vocabulary productively with confidence, their learning of words needs to be complex and deep. A single meeting of a word may start the process of learning, as Webb (2007) has shown in his experimental study, but the knowledge may be minimal, fragmented, imprecise, and not conducive for productive use. Three conditions appear to be central to effective vocabulary learning: repeated meetings, deep processing, and pushed output activities.

Repeated meetings of words in new contexts will consolidate the learning process (Nation, 2015). In addition, what happens at the time of first encountering the word is central to the quality of learning.

Deep processing of words is a second key element in vocabulary development. Finally, the learning process continues as words are activated productively through **pushed output activities**. This idea of pushing students to use the words they know, including newly acquired words from reading, is central to the type of vocabulary acquisition that can lead to use in writing. These three conditions—repeated meetings in context, deep processing, and pushed output—will now be discussed in more detail.

Repeated Meetings in Context

To develop a sufficient understanding of words so that they can be used in their writing, L2 students need to be exposed to target words repeatedly and in meaningful contexts (Nation, 2015). Although there is no point at which vocabulary learning is complete, Horst, Cobb, and Meara (1998) and Webb (2007) have suggested a threshold of ten encounters for developing a good understanding of new words. Repeated exposure to target words could occur during a single class session and extend over a series of classes, allowing students to retrieve or recall knowledge of previously encountered words as they update their knowledge of the ways that a word functions and behaves. Each new meeting of a target word contributes to the learning process, enabling a deeper and more precise understanding of the ways that the word appears and can be used in the language. One activity that encourages repetition of words is the **4-3-2 activity**, in which pairs of learners take turns speaking to each other on a topic of focus in class, first for four minutes, then for three minutes, and then for two minutes (see Nation & Gu, 2007: 76–77). The repetitive focus and shortened time have been shown to lead to efforts by the speakers to use words effectively, concisely, and accurately.

Deep Processing

The process of vocabulary development can also be improved if the quality of learning at the time of meeting is enhanced to promote deep processing of new words. Laufer and Hulstijn (2001) have proposed an **Involvement Load Hypothesis** to represent this process, with three variables affecting the involvement load of the student: need, search, and evaluation. First, *need* relates to how motivated the student is to learn the new word in terms of its perceived value or relevance. Second, *search* involves an attempt to discover the meaning of a new word, which could be through use of contextual clues, a dictionary, or guidance from classmates or the teacher. Third, *evaluation* considers the word's suitability in relation to other known words (for example, learning the world *rural* would be useful to students familiar with the word *urban*) which builds on the idea that word learning is shaped by the words already known and that some words will be more valued or useful than others. The combination of these three variables shapes the depth-of-word processing at the time of learning.

Pushed Output Activities

To encourage use of a broader range of words among their students, L2 writing instructors push students to activate a greater part of their receptive lexicon when writing—to use words newly learned while reading. **Pushed output** is accomplished through short controlled tasks such as sentence writing or paragraph writing, where students are given a topic or choice of topics and a selection of specific newly acquired target words to use. For example, in these types of guided tasks, students could be required to insert missing words in a text or on a diagram (Nation & Gu, 2007) as a stepping stone to less controlled forms of writing.

By adopting a view of pushed output as a central component of the vocabulary learning process, writing teachers can provide scaffolding, as needed, to assist students in introducing new words in writing. This could take the form of direct teaching of word forms, meanings, and uses, helping students to recognize that deep understanding of words is critical to being able to use them effectively in writing. The provision of support could address these questions raised by Coxhead (2007: 332) based on Nation's (2001: 327) framework:

- **form**: How is the word written and spelled?
- **form and meaning**: Which word form(s) can be used to express this meaning?
- **concepts and referents**: Which items can this concept refer to?
- **association**: Which other words can be used instead of this one?
- **grammatical function**: In what slots or positions must this word be used?
- **collocations**: Which words or types of words must be used with this one?
- **constraints of use**: Where, when, and how often can this word be used?

Pushed output tasks, thus, are a stepping stone for students toward more automatic use of new vocabulary in their writing. One documented form of pushed output proven to improve vocabulary use is portfolios (Ok, 2014), in which students produce and collate different forms of writing related to their learning process, with an interest in the *process* of writing rather than the *products* of writing. This enables a focus on vocabulary development that may not always be associated with portfolios. Portfolio writing, undertaken in and out of class, encourages L2 writers to use newly acquired words in compositions in a safe and supportive environment. In Ok's (2014) use of portfolios, the students reported on overall positive experience of vocabulary use through portfolio writing activities, as conveyed in student comments shown in Figure 5.4.

Figure 5.4: Experiences with Portfolio Writing in the Words of Students

- I used to look up words in the dictionary more often in the past, and words wouldn't come to my mind easily. Now, I'm better. I'm pleased with the progress I have made.
- Now, I'm more relaxed because the vocabulary I have learned helps me write more easily. I can see that I don't use simple words anymore.
- Now I see that my vocabulary has developed a lot, and I can be more selective in word choice. For instance, when I write an essay or a paragraph, I don't use every word that comes to my mind, but I try to choose the most suitable ones. I feel that I'm being more sensitive about which words to select as I write.
- As a student who got accustomed to the test technique, I have to say I found it difficult to write about the topics at the beginning of the course, but in time I realized that I took a long way in the use of vocabulary and grammar. The words I learned in the units helped me to select the right words which I needed to use.
- Keeping a portfolio has forced me to write. In time, I was aware of the fact that I had to put effort into it, and writing about every topic became a priority for me. It forced me to create a product each time I tried. I'm really satisfied with my progress. Especially my vocabulary has developed quite a lot. I tried to use the new words I learned each time I wrote about a topic. As I used the new words in each writing task in each unit, I could remember them whenever I needed. I can say that I can use English better now and express my thoughts more easily when I write. At the beginning of the school year I was afraid to put my ideas on paper.
- In this course, I got the opportunity to reflect the vocabulary I have learned into whatever I wrote. In time, I saw that I could remember some key vocabulary easily .... As the course progressed, I didn't need to use my dictionary very often. My vocabulary was limited when I started at the department, but I feel that I have learned quite a lot of useful vocabulary. I was always making simple sentences at first, but in time I started to make complex sentences.

Source: Ok, 2014, p. 58.

It's considered best practice for teachers to frequently introduce vocabulary at various stages of the writing process, including the planning, drafting, and feedback stages (Hayes, 2012; Hayes & Flower, 1980), so as to support their students as they write. Promoting lexical development in this process involves encouraging the use of vocabulary that have the correct form and meaning, which demonstrates students understanding the words, therefore allowing students to reach the threshold of knowledge required to confidently produce the words in their writing. When discussing preparing writing teachers to teach the vocabulary of academic prose, Coxhead and Byrd (2007) highlight the complexity and multifaceted nature associated with using new vocabulary in writing:

> Knowing a word to use it in writing involves at least understanding and expressing meaning in a range of contexts, spelling (and pronunciation for some people so that they might guess how to spell a word), regular grammatical patterns of occurrence, collocations or words that commonly occur with the word, word families, formality, word parts, and synonyms and opposites. (p. 132)

This depth of understanding can be built gradually over time through multiple encounters of the words in rich contexts. Teachers can promote vocabulary development during reading through more direct approaches to identifying target words and through activities focusing on aspects of word knowledge. By thematically linking reading to writing, teachers create more robust opportunities to focus on target words within meaningful contexts. In this way, vocabulary learning will improve their uptake in writing because students will see the relevance and the way they improve their writing.

Writing teachers can support students during pushed output by scaffolding to address any gaps in word knowledge that may be interfering with their use in writing. This could be associated with problematic aspects of vocabulary use such as correct use of **near synonyms** (i.e., semantically similar items), which have been noted as a common cause of lexical error in writing (Huang et al., 2019). An error can occur when students are unaware that the near synonyms do not share some collocates, as is the case with collocations of the near synonyms *refuse* and *reject*: we can say *refuse to leave* and *reject her* *request*, but not *reject to leave*. Other noted confusing sets of near synonyms potentially giving rise to error in use with collocations are: *ordinary-usual-common, destroy-ruin-spoil, scarce-rare-unusual, defeat-win-beat, sight-landscape-scenery, briefly-shortly-concisely, hard-difficult-tough, error-mistake-oversight, duty-job-task* and *obligation-responsibility-commitment* (Huang et al., 2019: 469).

As students become more familiar with words and gain experience using them in writing informed by feedback on their success, they will be more inclined to employ a larger range of words, with improved outcomes, as they continue with their overall writing development.

Key Points

1. Vocabulary learning is an incremental process, and students may need support using partially known words (see Chapter 1) in their writing because of the complexities associated with activating word knowledge.
2. L2 writing teachers can encourage students to use a wider range of words by exposing them to important academic words repeatedly in varied contexts and by facilitating deep understanding of the words. Both quantity and quality of vocabulary learning are important for L2 writers.
3. Activities that push students to use newly acquired words in controlled tasks can serve as a stepping stone to their use in subsequent compositions.

Sample Activities for the Classroom

Activity 1: Elementary School Level

You want to quickly improve your elementary school students' familiarity with and use of K1 words as this will form the foundation of all future writing. You encourage them to read graded readers for pleasure for 30 minutes each day at a level suited to their vocabulary knowledge. They should gradually work their way up levels within the graded readers. This activity exposes your students to commonly used words in a comprehensible and meaningful context. Each lesson commences with a fluency activity where they talk to each other in pairs for five minutes on what they have been reading and then write in a journal for ten minutes on their reflections on the reading. They should aim to write more words each day within the ten minutes. The teacher occasionally reads the students' journals but does not make corrections. The journal encourages activation of words in writing that they encountered while reading for pleasure.

Activity 2: High School Level

In a high school classroom, the teacher uses language- and meaning-focused activities (Nation & Yamamoto, 2012) to encourage retention of K2 words that can then be activated in writing. The target K2 words are:

anxious, argue, benefit, borrow, confuse, diet, ignore, innocent, polite, success

1. For the language focus, the teacher gives students in small groups sentences with K2 words underlined and asks to discuss the meanings, using the context as a clue where needed. They then check this with a dictionary. Here the focus is on language (i.e., vocabulary).
2. In the meaning-focused follow-up stage, the teacher asks students comprehension questions about the text that tests their knowledge of the target K2 words. Here the focus is on meaning.

3. The teacher then provides the students with new sentences with spaces for the target K2 words and asks them, working in groups, to put a K2 word in each space. This task assesses learning of these words in a controlled, productive way.
4. Based on this series of tasks, students are given a writing task where they are to use five of the K2 words on a topic of their choice. This forced-output task consolidates prior learning, allowing the words to be available for future activation in writing.

Activity 3: University Level

Students in a 12-week program are given a list of 20 target words at the start of each week. The words are taken from K1, K2, AWL, or a disciplinary technical word list, as determined by the language level of the students and their language learning purpose.

Each week has a different thematic approach (e.g., inventions, ancient civilizations, eco-tourism) with reading input including target words that are in boldface, underlined, or highlighted to encourage noticing. Listening input is also provided. A direct focus on vocabulary—form, meaning, collocations, etc.—reinforces learning.

Forced-output tasks such as sentence writing encourage productive use of the target words. At the end of each week, students complete a vocabulary test involving gap-fill and paragraph writing of the 20 target items. Students receive feedback on their performance as part of a formative feedback process to inform future learning. In future weeks, the target words are revisited in new contexts to consolidate learning. During Weeks 6 and 12, students are given longer writing tasks to draw on vocabulary that has become internalized in their productive lexicon.

Tasks and Discussion Questions for Teachers

1. It is generally accepted that some of the words L2 students know and can recognize when they read do not appear in our writing. There can be various reasons for this. However, if a student who can understand simple language is unable to write anything even with encouragement from the teacher, what might be a good way to help the student to get started?
2. Some students may have developed effective strategies for vocabulary learning that result in effective use of new words in writing. How could we encourage sharing of such strategies among a class of writers?
3. Pushed output is seen as a key to activating known words in writing, yet it requires scaffolding to assist students with the process. What are some specific pushed output activities and scaffolding you could apply in your L2 writing class?

Chapter 6

Treatment of Errors in Vocabulary Use

GUIDING QUESTIONS

1. How should writing teachers view vocabulary errors in L2 writing?
2. What types of vocabulary errors appear in L2 writing?
3. How can writing teachers respond to vocabulary errors?

This chapter examines the nature of vocabulary errors and how they should be viewed in light of current understandings of SLA and L2 vocabulary development. The discussion then moves to the reasons for vocabulary error occurrence in L2 writing and the types of errors teachers find. Approaches to responding to vocabulary errors in writing are then discussed, including coding. The chapter then considers the types of writing that are not particularly well suited to vocabulary error treatment.

The Nature of Vocabulary Errors

Errors in L2 writing are a natural process of acquiring a second language and reflective of students going through different stages in their language development (Ferris, 2011). Errors in productive word use may provide an insight into students' developmental stage of language acquisition, as suggested in the SLA concept of **interlanguage** (Selinker, 1972), which shows how errors are evidence of learning, and not displays of failed learning.

In the case of vocabulary errors, Henriksen (1999) has presented L2 vocabulary development as being on a continuum from partial to precise (see Chapter 1). For students to make progress in their L2 writing, they need opportunities to activate knowledge of newly acquired words and to receive guidance and feedback relative to vocabulary use. Some students will be more willing to take chances, resulting in higher risk of error incidence, but a more cautious learner might use a more limited lexicon to avoid making errors. Error frequency, therefore, can reflect the attitude that learners take to their writing development. Thus, teachers are encouraged to find out how students feel about making lexical errors (how much risk they will take) and then explain their expectations for vocabulary use in the writing class.

Causes of Vocabulary Errors

Research into the causes of lexical error in second language writing has tended to distinguish conceptually between two main types of error: **interlingual**, concerning errors caused by interference of the L1 on the L2, and **intralingual**, representing errors caused by weakness in understandings within the L2 (Carrió-Pastor & Mestre-Mestre, 2014). With interlingual errors, transfer of knowledge and rules from the L1 can result in incorrect decisions made in the L2 with word form (spelling), word choice and/or word use. Rauser (2017) sheds light on the appearance of interlingual errors of Czech learners of English. As an example, a student has wrongly used the word *chef* (instead of *boss)* in a writing task (p. 219):

> *I work part-time in an office for a marketing company....My chef is strict and he gives me a lot of work, ...but my chef is fair and I like him.*

The error is likely due to the association made by the learner with the Czech word *šéf,* which means "boss." As the learner develops a deeper understanding of English, this interlingual error would be expected to disappear.

Transfer of lexical knowledge from the L1 to the L2 can be a positive process, contributing to correct use of L2 words, and can be a negative process, leading to misunderstandings of word form, meaning, and/or use. In the case of intralingual errors, the cause is weaknesses in understanding within the new language (Hashimoto & Egbert, 2019). Intralingual lexical errors include some well-documented categories. One key aspect is **orthographic regularity,** which is the extent to which a word's spelling follows the norms of the language (think of verbs that are referred to as *irregular).* This occurs with simple past tense forms that typically are signaled with *-ed* endings, where this regular form is not evident in *found, sought,* and *thought.* Thus, errors such as *thinked* and *seeked* would be likely tied to orthographical irregularity. Another example occurs with superlatives, where the form *-est* as in *fastest* and *kindest* is typically overgeneralized to forms like *bestest* and *worstest* (instead of *best* and *worst*).

Morphological regularity is another factor. This concerns the complexity and transparency of inflectional and derivational features (including prefixes, suffixes, and inflectional endings) because morphological features that are less regular are considered more difficult to learn. This is evident in the multiple forms of negative prefixes used in English (e.g., *happy-unhappy, possible-impossible, responsible-irresponsible,* etc.), leading to possible errors in the production of words in writing.

Interestingly, **word length** can also be a factor because longer words put a greater demand on the learner. Longer words tend to be multisyllabic, making them more challenging to learn. The fact that many of the technical terms and academic words students may encounter in school are borrowings from Latin and Greek (e.g., *photosynthesis, methodology, domestication,* *geography, atmospheric*) means that L2 writers will need to learn more about English words parts (morphology), something that is less necessary when it comes to words such as *cat, help*, and *keep*.

Laufer (1988) has discussed **synformy**, which describes words that have a similar (but not the same) form but different meanings. Obviously, these are challenging for L2 students (although not only L2 students). Examples include *affect-effect, quite-quiet,* and *simulate-stimulate*. In the case of *affect-effect*, as these word forms may be acquired at the same time, the possibility for their misuse in writing is enhanced as evident in *This had a negative* *affect* (effect) *on my motivation*.

Laufer (1989) has used the term **deceptive transparency** to refer to words that are confusing because of their form. Consider how the word *infallible* may be wrongly mistaken to be a form of the word *fall*, as in *in+fall+ible*, which would suggest a meaning of "something that cannot fall," whereas its meaning is more along the lines of "incapable of making a mistake or being wrong." If L2 learners process these words incorrectly when they first encounter them, they may, in turn, use them incorrectly in writing and may produce a vocabulary error.

Types of Vocabulary Errors Appearing in Student Writing

Research has provided some insights on the types of lexical errors found in L2 writing. Erkaya (2012) found that errors in word choice were the most common lexical errors made in comparison/contrast essays of first-year university students in Turkey. Some of these errors interfered with clarity of meaning. Others, including Darus and Subramaniam (2009) and Kirkgöz (2010), have also noted frequent errors in word choice in L2 writing, although in these studies, the errors did not affect text comprehensibility. The extent to which errors affect the reader experience shapes how teachers respond to errors, with more attention directed to those that confuse.

In a detailed study of vocabulary use in L2 writing, Hemchua and Schmitt (2006) reported on lexical errors found in the writing of persuasive compositions of 300–350 words of third-year university students in Thailand. The topic of these compositions was the advantages of urban or country living. Their study also found frequent word choice errors and included both single- and multiword items, as well as errors related to level of formality (register), incorrect meanings, lack of or under-specification (not clear what the writer meant), and clear interference from the L1. Figure 6.1 shows a number of categories of lexical error with examples of errors (underlined) and suggested correct form (in brackets) sourced from Hemchua and Schmitt (2006).

Figure 6.1: Types of Lexical Errors in Writing

Word choice (using the wrong word or words)

- One word: (*But country people are sincere and share* [*generous*].) (*The city is grown* [*developed*].) (*I think the city has good communication* [*transportation/public transport*] *such as a lot of buses.*) (*We have modern equipment* [*appliances*] *in our house.*)
- Two or more words: (*They will travel by cart or by legs* [*on foot*].) (*He said that my mother and he had mutual consensus* [*reached a mutual consensus*].)

Formality (informal use of words): (*We can communicate with people and get* [*gain/acquire*] *knowledge from other countries by using computers.*)

Incorrect meaning from that intended: (*You will get up* [*wake up*] *in the morning because of the sound of birds.*)

Underspecification (where ideas need to be more fully developed lexically): (*Although cars in the country are lower* [*Although there are fewer cars in the country/Although car numbers in the country are lower*].)

Interference from L1: In this case, for a Thai student (*We have to find a car to bring us go to* [*bring us to*] *the hospital.*)

Source: Examples from Hemchua & Schmitt, 2006, pp. 9–20.

Errors with Collocations and Lexical Bundles

Because collocations and lexical bundles are shaped by rules of grammar and usage, they are particularly challenging for students to acquire and use confidently. Nevertheless, more advanced learners have been shown to successfully use collocations and lexical bundles, as identified by Nesselhauf (2005: 68):

solve a problem	*have a right*	*have a problem*
have a chance	*get an impression*	*have time*
commit a crime	*answer a question*	*do work*

When those learners did make errors using collocations and lexical bundles, they tended to be similar to those listed (Nesselhauf, 2005: 66):

- *break a ritual* (*change a ritual* would have been more appropriate)
- *reanimate your breathing* (*get your breath back* would have been more appropriate)
- *do a turn* (*turn around* would have been more appropriate)
- *hang on the telephone* (*spend a long time on the telephone* would have been more appropriate)

When it comes to the task of responding to errors in collocations and lexical bundles in writing, it is a manual process for instructors, one unaided by technology. To address this issue, Park et al. (2008) developed **AwkChecker**, an online tool that helps identify (and correct) errors in use of collocations and lexical bundles. A similar product is **AccurIT** (Grami, 2020) that is designed to guide students with correct use of collocations and lexical bundles in their writing.

Feedback on Vocabulary Use in Writing

Feedback provides a valuable opportunity for students to gain information on the success of vocabulary use in their writing. Providing students with feedback on errors in word use will facilitate their progression along the partial-precise continuum (see Chapter 1) because it enables them to understand how their choices were interpreted by readers, thereby leading them to deepen their word knowledge as they revise their writing. This is a good way for L2 writing teachers to shape the quality of student writing as a product, as well as the quality of student learning as a process (Raimes, 1983; Zamel, 1985).

Coxhead (2006) suggests involving learners in the process of tailoring feedback on vocabulary use in writing by asking them what aspects they are most concerned about:

- Do they seek feedback on their range of vocabulary, on accuracy of form, meaning, and use, or on alternative word choices available?
- How would they like the feedback and revision process to operate?
- Do they want to engage deeply, as language learners, in the process in an inductive way, or do they seek a more direct approach to correction from the teacher?

Teachers need to decide whether peer review by students should be a component in the feedback process. These questions shed light on the variability surrounding feedback processes with vocabulary use.

A key component of vocabulary feedback is deciding which words to focus on. If the writing task involves **target words** as part of its design, then feedback can be provided on positive and negative dimensions of form, meaning, and use for these words. If the focus of the writing involves use of collocations, the feedback process can extend student understandings of the acceptable or appropriate collocations in the chosen subject area. If the focus is on lexical bundles, students will want to know if they are using these correctly in terms of meaning and tone. They may, for example, ask their teacher if the lexical bundles give the writing a native-like feel (see Salazar, 2014). In this case, it's necessary for teachers to talk about lexical bundles within the context of the type of writing students have been assigned. Students can learn, for example, that overuse of a small number of lexical bundles may give their writing an odd feel, a problem also associated with use of collocations (Antle, 2018). Thus, feedback on vocabulary can help students reflect on broader issues of writing quality, appropriate models of writing, and disciplinary expectations.

Teachers are familiar with the use of coding to identify errors when giving feedback in L2 writing (see Ferris, 2011). Although it's efficient for teachers, codes can lead to misunderstanding by students. To address this concern, teachers should train students on how they plan to use the codes (and what they mean) before using them. Toward this end, Coxhead (2006) has suggested using something like the chart provided in Figure 6.2:

Figure 6.2: Sample Chart of Vocabulary Error Codes

Error Type	Error Code	Example of Error	Details Regarding Error
wrong word	WW	*One way to protect disease is vaccinations.*	prevent would be a suitable substitute for protect
wrong meaning	WM	*One type of bacteria is a virus.*	a virus is not a type of bacteria
spelling	SP	*Medical staff are trained to asist patients.*	correct spelling is assist
wrong collocation	W/COLL	*Some patients may have specific dietary demands.*	should be dietary needs or dietary requirements
formality level	FORMAL / INFORMAL	*There are heaps of beds in a communal hospital ward.*	many would be more formal than the colloquial heaps of
word family	WF	*Patients may be required to recovery at home.*	should be recover (verb) rather than recovery (noun)
grammar	GR	*In the future, new treatments may develop.*	should be the passive form be developed rather than the active form develop

Source: Adapted from Coxhead, 2006, p. 130. Used with permission of Cengage Learning.

To show how this works, Figure 6.3 shows a sample student text marked with the codes. The error has been highlighted with underlining and a code entered next to the error.

With training, students will be able to reflect on the nature of the vocabulary error and self-correct in a subsequent draft. It's not a perfect solution and is obviously dependent on many factors (familiarity with rules of grammar and usage, understanding of formality, and overall vocabulary size, etc.).

Although feedback on vocabulary use in writing may result in immediate correction of the error in a subsequent draft of the writing, is that sufficient? Does that mean the student understands and will not make the same mistake again? Will the student feel encouraged by the feedback and continue to take the risk to use the word in the future, or will they not take the risk? What is the longer-term effect of receiving feedback on vocabulary?

Figure 6.3: Student Text with Lexical Errors Marked for Correction

The Role of Our Health System

Our health system is very important in society to keep us all healthy. One way to protect **[WW]** disease is vaccinations. This is used particularly with young children and the elderly. They can protect us against harmful effects of infection from bacteria. One type of bacteria is a virus. **[WM]** These can be more difficult to vaccinate against. When unwell, we rely on doctors and nurses, as well as specialists. Medical staff are trained to asist **[SP]** patients. In some cases, patients are admitted to hospital. Some patients may have specific dietary demands. **[W/COLL]** There may be options for single rooms or large wards. There are heaps of **[INFORMAL]** beds in a communal hospital ward. Hospital stays can be quite short, especially if there is a need for care of other sick people. Patients may be required to recovery **[WF]** at home. Our health care system is constantly improving. In the future, new treatments may develop. **[GR]** That could further improve the health of our population.

Source: Based on an anonymous unpublished student text used with permission.

Some forms of writing may not require or be suited to feedback on error for a variety of reasons. Keeping a vocabulary log or journal, for example, is often regarded as a student-centered activity not involving teacher feedback (Diaz, 2015). Too great a focus on errors can detract students from the purpose of writing.

This does not suggest that teachers should not give feedback. Learners may like their writing to be seen and read by the teacher. The teacher could respond as an interested reader with comments and questions about ideas discussed in the writing and encourage future writing. Sometimes the L2 writing teacher is helping the learner by ignoring vocabulary errors in writing.

Clearly, development of word knowledge is incremental and complex. Teachers need to be aware that feedback is only one component of the learning program and not a substitute for it. Research shows that vocabulary development benefits from a wide range of incidental and direct approaches.

Key Points

1. The production of lexical errors in L2 writing are natural processes in the language learning process. Making errors needs to be viewed as a component of the learning process and as an opportunity to provide feedback on use.
2. Errors in vocabulary use in L2 writing can be the result of L1 interference or as the result of weaknesses in knowledge within the L2. Intralexical errors refers to errors associated specifically with features of vocabulary use.
3. Some types of writing may not be suited to vocabulary error correction, in which case the teacher may need to respond to the writing in other ways such as an interested reader or by encouraging longer or more detailed writing.

Tasks and Discussion Questions for Teachers

1. As a writing teacher, you may find yourself reading through student compositions (these could be paragraphs, essays, reports, poems or stories, etc.) and noticing errors with use of words. There could be a range of types of errors. Should you correct them all for the students, or approach it another way? What is your thinking of good ways to approach this task, so that the time spent by you (and your students) is not wasted?
2. Monitor what happens once feedback is provided on writing. Does it inform a next draft of the writing? Does it reduce errors in the next draft? More important, what impact does error correction have on longer-term use of vocabulary, as exhibited in subsequent writing?
3. Consider what types of writing lend themselves well to providing feedback on vocabulary use. Are there other aspects of writing that would not be suited for feedback on vocabulary use? If so, what types of writing and what would be the rationale for withholding this feedback?

Chapter 7

Technological Applications

GUIDING QUESTIONS

1. What types of technology can inform vocabulary instruction?
2. What information can technology provide?
3. How can this information inform the use of vocabulary in writing?

This chapter explores technologies that can assist with the development of the lexical component of L2 writing, in particular, patterns of word use including collocations. The chapter then looks at the use of corpora and software programs to identify the types of lexical analysis data teachers and students can use either online or on a local computer.

Considerations on the Use of Technology

We can view technology as a tool for improving our understanding of the use of vocabulary in language production. With advances in technology, our ability to generate information on vocabulary use has improved, with enhanced scope for generating quite specific data.

One application of technology is the generation of word frequency lists, on the basis that the most frequently occurring words deserve the most attention from a teaching and learning perspective. Leech (2011) explains the significance of frequency in vocabulary use with data showing that the most frequently occurring 50 words of English account for 40 percent of running words (tokens) in written language, rising to 85 percent at 3,000 words and 92 percent at 10,000 words. Thus, not all words are equal.

Another area of interest in the use of technology is to provide learners with exposure to words in rich and varied contexts, which can be more controlled using technology than through intensive or extensive reading. This approach, discussed in Boulton (2017), would see students exposed to lexical patterns, collocations, and lexical bundles tailored for their learning program and representative of authentic uses of language.

Introducing new technologies requires investments of time and resources and involves both teachers and students in a new learning process. Once mastery of the technology is attained, there is the scope for continued benefit, but this may require a sustained level of teacher and student commitment. It can be assumed that student experiences of the technology will be variable and student attrition from a voluntary program can be evident.

Corpora

Technological advancements with computers and computing applications have seen developments in the type and quality of tools and resources available related to the use of vocabulary in writing. One area of development has been with computer-based corpora. These are collections in electronic form of texts, written and/or spoken, that are examples of how language is used in society. A corpus, through its design, is thus a window into language use. A corpus can be specialized, as in a corpus of scientific writing, or general, as in a corpus of written and spoken English. Corpora tend to be divided into sections, for example:

- spoken (monologues, dialogues, unscripted, scripted), such as conversations and speeches
- written, such as letters, news stories, novels, research articles, and student writing

They can be designed around subject areas, such as the arts, economics, science, and law. They can also be specialist corpora, for example:

- expert writing, such as engineering research papers
- student writing, such as writing samples

One by-product of corpus analysis is the development of corpus-based dictionaries such as the COBUILD dictionary, which provides learners with word definitions as well as examples of the target word in context extracted from a corpus. Frankenberg-Garcia (2012), in a study of university students in Portugal enrolled in an undergraduate tourism degree program, arrived at findings that suggest that dictionary definitions coupled with multiple corpus-sourced examples of the word in context promote vocabulary learning. However, corpus examples alone can be problematic from a vocabulary learning perspective if the sample text includes words of lower frequency than the target word, thus presenting the learner with obstacles to comprehension. These corpora are particularly useful in the context of improving the vocabulary component of writing:

- **British National Corpus (BNC)** (2007) is a collection of samples of written and spoken language representing more than 100 million words. The written section, representing 90 percent of the corpus, covers a wide range of genres and text types. The spoken section, representing 10 percent of the corpus, covers a wide range of spoken language contexts. Available at http://www.natcorp.ox.ac.uk

- **Corpus of Contemporary American English (COCA)** (Davies, 2008–2020) has more than one billion words, including these genres: spoken, fiction, magazines, newspapers, academic, general web, blog web, and TV/movies. Available at https://www.english-corpora.org/coca
- **Michigan Corpus of Upper-level Student Papers (MICUSP)** (2009) is an electronic collection of papers written by students at the University of Michigan, covering a range of text types and academic disciplines. Available at http://micusp.elicorpora.info
- **British Academic Writing in English (BAWE)** corpus is an electronic collection of texts produced by undergraduate and graduate students in a range of disciplines in the United Kingdom. Available at http://www2.warwick.ac.uk/fac/soc/al/research/collect/bawe
- **International Corpus of Learner English (ICLE)** is an electronic collection of writing by upper-intermediate to advanced learners from a range of L1 backgrounds. Available at http://www.uclouvain.be/en-cecl-icle.html
- **International Corpus of English (ICE)** (Nelson, 2016–2020) is an electronic collection of corpora from a range of participating countries provided by local research teams. Each corpus contains one million words of written and spoken (or in some cases written only) language. Available at http://ice-corpora.net/ice

Comprehensive lists of specialized corpora are compiled by:

- Corpus Resource Database (CoRD) (2020). Corpora finder hosted by the Research Unit for the Study of Variation, Contacts and Change in English (VARIENG). Available at http://www.helsinki.fi/varieng/CoRD/corpora/corpusfinder
- Weisser (2020). Specialized corpora. Available at http://martinweisser.org/corpora_site/spec_corpora.html

Comprehensive lists of learner corpora are compiled by:

- Centre for English Corpus Linguistics (2020) at Université Catholique de Louvain. Available at https://uclouvain.be/en/research-institutes/ilc/cecl/learner-corpora-around-the-world.html
- Common Language Resources and Technology Infrastructure (CLARIN) (2020). Available at https://www.clarin.eu/resource-families/L2-corpora

Building Your Own Corpus

The range of specialized corpora and web-based vocabulary analysis tools will continue to increase with time. L2 teachers who are interested in this aspect of L2 writing should keep up to date on the most useful corpora and tools for their students and should share this knowledge with their students; time spent analyzing writing will be most valuable if the information provided is well tailored to the students' specific learning needs. For those wishing to construct a corpus of expert writing or a corpus of learner writing, useful guides on this process include:

- Corpus Linguistics (2020). DIY corpora: Building and using your own corpora. Available at https://www.lancaster.ac.uk/fss/courses/ling/corpus/blue/diy_top.htm
- Reppen (2010). Building a corpus. Available at https://www.routledgehandbooks.com/doi/10.4324/9780203856949.ch3
- Sketch Engine (2020). Create a corpus from the web. Available at https://www.sketchengine.eu/guide/create-a-corpus-from-the-web

Web-Based Resources

There are a range of web-based resources available for researcher, teacher, and student analysis of the lexical component of writing:

- **Paul Nation's** website provides a range of vocabulary- and reading-related resources, including vocabulary lists and vocabulary analysis programs. See https://www.wgtn.ac.nz/lals/resources/paul-nations-resources
- **Word and Phrase** (Davies, 2013) is a tool for analyzing word- and phrase-oriented features of electronic texts, operating from within the COCA website. Available at https://www.english-corpora.org/coca/
- **AntCon** (Anthony, 2019) is a corpus analysis toolkit for concordancing and lexical bundle analysis, in addition to key word and word frequency analysis. This software is suitable for classroom purposes, particularly in the creation of concordance tables. Available through https://www.laurenceanthony.net/software/antconc/
- **NetCollo** (Huang & Tsao, 2020) is an online corpus-based collocation tool that enables users to test whether a combination is possible in English, learn semantically related correct combinations, and explore semantically related miscollocations. Available at http://www.netcollo.info
- **Web-Based L2 Syntactic Complexity Analyzer** (Ai, 2020) is a tool for analyzing the syntactic complexity of texts, which uses 14 different measures covering length of production units, amounts of coordination, amounts of subordination, degree of phrasal sophistication, and overall sentence complexity. Available at https://aihaiyang.com/software/
- **UAM Computer Tools** (O'Donnell, 2019) is for those building corpora that require coding. Available at http://www.corpustool.com

- **Coh-Metrix**, reported in Graesser et al. (2004), is an advanced computational tool that enables analysis of a range of features of texts including word characteristics, sentence characteristics, and discourse relationships between ideas in text. Available at http://cohmetrix.memphis.edu/cohmetrixhome/documentation_indices.html
- **TAALES (Tool for the Automatic Analysis of Lexical Sophistication)** reported in Kyle, Crossley, and Berger (2018) enables sophisticated analysis of lexical features including n-grams, word associations, contextual diversity measures, and word range scores. Available at https://www.linguisticanalysistools.org/taales.html
- **Compleat Lexical Tutor** (Cobb, 2020), often referred to as **Lextutor**, is a web-based online analysis package with a range of tools and programs to enable analysis of the lexical component of texts (available at https://www.lextutor.ca). This online resource includes analysis tools that teachers and their learners can use to inform the development of the lexical component of writing:
- **N-Gram**: to generate concordance lines for target words in a sample of writing. N-gram refers to a sequence of words coded numerically (i.e., number of words in the chain), such as *hard work* (2-gram), *to sum up* (3-gram), *from time to time* (4-gram), and *to tell you the truth* (5-gram).
- **Concordance**: to generate concordance lines for target words in a selection of corpora. A concordance is a listing of each occurrence of a word in a text or a corpus, presented with the words surrounding it. The number of words appearing in a concordance line on each side (left and right) of the target word can be set.
- **VocabProfile**: to generate a lexical profile of a sample of writing, including the percentage of words used from different word frequency and specialization lists as well as type-token ratio reporting. Word lists widely used with VocabProfile include the BNC lists (K1 and K2), the AWL, and BNC/COCA lists.

Software Programs

The development of online programs to analyze word use in corpora and in single texts has equipped researchers and text developers with the means to identify patterns of vocabulary use in both general and specific language contexts. These electronic software programs are particularly useful for this:

- **WordSmith Tools** (Scott, 2020) is a software package that can be used for construction of concordance tables and word lists and for key word searches within a text or corpus. Available at https://www.lexically.net/wordsmith
- **MonoConc Pro** is a web-based concordance tool that enables the user to retrieve all examples of a word or phrase (or part of a word) from a text or corpus. Available at http://athel.com/index.html
- **VocabProfile** (Heatley, Nation, & Coxhead, 2002) is a software package appearing within Compleat Lexical Tutor. Figure 7.1 shows the vocabulary profile for a student essay.

The VocabProfile report for this text of 234 tokens (or running words) indicates that 93.59 percent of tokens appear in the K1 word list, 1.71 percent of tokens appear in the K2 word list, 3.85 percent of tokens appear in the AWL, and 0.85 percent of tokens do not appear in these three word lists.

Figure 7.1: Sample VocabProfile Data for a Student Essay

Wordlist	Lexical Coverage (%)
K1 Words	93.59
K2 Words	1.71
AWL Words	3.85
Other Words	0.85
Total	100.00

Baseword Lists

Baseword lists have been developed to group words by frequency of occurrence in the language and by specialization. They can be designed around word family groups that allow for reporting of word use. Figure 7.2 shows word family entries for three baseword lists (K1, K2, and AWL) indicating word family groupings.

To tailor for young learners, word lists have been developed at 250-word intervals reflective of the spoken language of young language users, enabling more sensitive reporting of vocabulary use than is provided by 1,000-word intervals. Figure 7.3 shows examples of items in the Kids01 to Kids09 word lists.

Figure 7.2: Examples of Word Family Listings in Baseword Lists

K1 List	K2 List	Academic Word List
progress	*imagine*	*constrain*
progressed	*imagining*	*constrained*
progresses	*imagines*	*constraining*
progressing	*imagined*	*constrains*
progressive	*imagination*	*constraint*
progressively	*imaginations*	*constraints*
	imaginative	*unconstrained*
	imaginary	

Figure 7.3: Items in Kids01 to Kids09 Word Lists

Kids01	Kids02	Kids03
friend	*eye*	*coat*
from	*face*	*cone*
fun	*far*	*cookie*
game	*fast*	*couple*
Kids04	**Kids05**	**Kids06**
surprise	*army*	*sunburn*
tall	*arrow*	*sunglasses*
tear	*balloon*	*swallow*
tennis	*bark*	*target*
Kids07	**Kids08**	**Kids09**
butcher	*vegetable*	*buffalo*
camera	*waist*	*burgle*
candle	*waste*	*camel*
capital	*western*	*carnival*

Baseword lists are used in conjunction with VocabProfile to enable reporting of vocabulary use in a corpus or a single text.

Concordancing and Collocation Clusters

Concordance tables provide data in the form of concordance lines, where the key word or target word appears in its immediate context, with a certain number of words appearing each side, as shown in Figure 7.4 for the words *protect* and *prevent.*

Concordancing has been used in the construction of dictionaries such as COBUILD to include authentic uses of words, for sociolinguistic research purposes to capture social uses of language, and to inform language teaching and learning.

The COCA online site allows for generation of collocation clusters listed in decreasing order of frequency for target words.

Figure 7.4: Concordance Lines for *protect* and *prevent*

are introducing new security measures in order to PROTECT their systems and as well as their

growing number of countries must take measures to PROTECT citizens and visitors from the threat of

environments. The Woodlands (regulated to PROTECT ecological condition) and the North

make way for the galloping new constructions. To PROTECT this city's priceless urban heritage from

led a passion and desire amongst Maori to defend, PROTECT and assert their Maori identity. The

apoptosis. In a screen for small molecules that PROTECT cells from ER stress induced apoptosis

States. It would also allow the Partnership to PROTECT the natural resources by gauging the use

a term that symbolizes a variety of barriers that PREVENT qualified individuals from advancing

individual, the meditation monk teachers help to PREVENT notions of the Buddha's greatness from

remedies) employed the house as a device to PREVENT ill fortune, to promote health and prosper

Despite decades of intensive research efforts to PREVENT mold, modern buildings continue to suffer

programs which would not only possibly help PREVENT couples from being ignorant of the essence

resolution has exploded with innovative ways to PREVENT conflict and resolve disagreements.

signal at around 1Hz frequency has been tried to PREVENT bubble generation while producing

Source: Compleat Lexical Tutor Online Concordancer (Cobb, 2020).

Data-Driven Learning

Data on vocabulary use can be utilized in two ways: indirectly, when the data are extracted by researchers and materials developers, and directly, when data are extracted and used by teachers and students (Römer, 2008). The latter, direct applications, are described as **data-driven learning (DDL)**, where the use of technology allows students, with teacher guidance, to access and use corpus data. In this model of learning, students utilize computer programs and software to generate data that relate specifically to their language needs, with particular relevance to improving vocabulary use as part of overall writing development.

Yilmaz (2017), exploring learner perceptions on the effects of DDL on vocabulary learning, found that most students reported that this first instance on using concordances helped them to learn the meanings of unfamiliar vocabulary items and that they appreciated the ways in which target words appear in collocations. Overall, concordance data, tailored for the writing task being attempted, assisted the students with ideas development in their writing. Although student experiences with the technology were variable, including some negative perceptions of its value, most of the students responded that they would value the opportunity to access concordance data in future writing tasks.

In a writing program with civil engineering students, Otto (2021) compiled data on vocabulary use in published writing to identify target words to be the focus of DDL activities. The researcher compiled an expert corpus of texts written by practicing engineers, including geotechnical reports, transportation reports, structural reports, water resources reports, environmental reports, and technical memos. The researcher also compiled a corpus of student writing with the inclusion of technical reports, technical memos, and laboratory reports. She compared the use of target vocabulary items associated with civil engineering to determine which were deemed problematic for her student group. The comparison included these aspects (Otto, 2021: 38):

- Word frequency (using the key word analysis tool of AntConc): This step looked at whether there was a significant difference in frequency of usage.
- Grammatical category (using the concordance tool of AntConc): This step involved scanning concordance lines to compare how a word was used grammatically.
- Collocations (using the collocates tool of AntConc): This step compared the top collocates and looked for differences in the types of words.
- Lexical bundles (using the clusters/n-grams tool of AntConc): This step compared use of three- and four-word bundles.
- Function (using the concordance tool of AntConc): Function was compared by reading concordance lines, looking at the top collocations and bundles in context, and noting the meanings conveyed and the apparent purpose for using the word.

Huang and Tsao (2019) report on a program designed to detect collocational errors in student writing using what they term an **online collocation explorer**, which provides a model of correct collocational use. Teachers can use this online collocation explorer in addition to providing feedback. The researchers were interested in helping students distinguish between correct collocations (e.g., *state truth, state fact*) from other combinations that are not correct (e.g., *say fact, say truth*). The research team utilized a web-based tool called NetCollo (Huang & Tsao, 2020) that they developed, using data from a reference corpus, to explore combinations such as verb + noun (e.g., *conduct research*) and adjective + noun (e.g., *heavy rain*). Students could use this tool to check whether their collocations are correct. Teachers can use NetCollo to generate lists of co-occurring words that students can refer to and learn from. To illustrate this process of error checking and guidance, a student has used the collocation *attain agreement* in a composition on the topic of "Should advertising of alcohol be permitted?" as follows:

> I don't think we can easily attain agreement in society on this important question.

This student could then generate data related to this collocation through NetCollo to test its suitability and view other collocation options available with each word (*attain* and *agreement*).

Technology can promote learner-centered vocabulary development in writing and is particularly suited to doctoral students who have the time and level of commitment to ensure the learning effort is rewarded with tangible benefits in terms of writing quality. Lee and Swales (2006) report on an approach adopted at the English Language Institute within the University of Michigan with a small group of doctoral students in an EAP program. The program was designed to promote rhetorical consciousness-raising by exposing learners to writing in a range of disciplines and encouraging them to be informed by writing in their own disciplinary area through concordance data generated from corpora. Rather than presenting students with concordance lines of words preselected by the teacher, the responsibility for learning was placed with the students. This required training in use of the concordance program (WordSmith Tools) with a collection of corpora. Fitting in with an ethnographic perspective of writing (Johns, 1997) in which students are encouraged to research language use in their disciplinary area, the course titled Exploring Your Own Discourse World required a high level of student commitment, reflecting the investment component attached to independent learning modes.

In a similar approach and with a much larger student body, Chen and Flowerdew (2018) report on the introduction of a DDL initiative with doctoral students from different disciplines in Hong Kong. A series of workshops trained students how to use the software (AntConc) with the BNC corpus and how to generate collocation and concordance data. They were then given guidance with the means to construct discipline specific corpora of research articles representing expert corpora in their area of research. Thus, they had the capacity to explore language use in their disciplinary area with reference to expert writing, which would serve as a model or resource for their individual language development.

With both approaches discussed here, the intent is for students to explore vocabulary use in their discipline as an insider rather than as an outside observer (Johns, 1997). In doing so, students can transition from novice to expert, representing movement from the periphery to the center in terms of membership of the discourse community (i.e., community of students, scholars, and teachers) in the disciplinary area—something that is particularly important for doctoral students seeking recognition and acceptance from peers in their chosen field.

Key Points

1. There are a range of corpora, lexical analysis programs, and other tools that can provide insights into vocabulary use in expert writing and in L2 writing.
2. Published texts (including books and journal articles) can be used as a model of expert writing to inform the writing of L2 students.
3. Students will require training if they are expected to use computer-generated data on vocabulary use in writing.

Tasks and Discussion Questions for Teachers

1. When considering use of technology in the language classroom, not all teachers come with the same levels of technical competence. It should not be seen as an achievement that the technology simply worked; surely, the aim should be for learning to occur. Given that not all language teachers will feel the same way about technology in the classroom, how would you like to see decisions made with schools and universities about use of technology when it comes to writing tasks?
2. Run a lexical analysis of a L2 writing sample from one of your students using the VocabProfile tool of **Compleat Lexical Tutor**, using one of the profilers available at https://www.lextutor.ca/vp. Consider how the analysis profile could inform vocabulary development in your students' writing.
3. Create a concordance line for a target word useful for your L2 learners, using **WordSmith Tools**, **AntConc**, or another concordance maker. Consider how this information on vocabulary use could be utilized in a L2 writing context.

Chapter 8

Fostering Independent Learning of Vocabulary

GUIDING QUESTIONS

1. What does "autonomy in learning" mean?
2. How can learner autonomy be fostered in terms of vocabulary use in writing?
3. What are the concerns that teachers face when introducing autonomy in the L2 writing classroom?

This chapter presents the case for fostering independent learning of vocabulary for use in writing. Dealing with learner autonomy in the concluding chapter of this book may suggest that this concept is an afterthought or is situated at the periphery of mainstream pedagogy, but this is not the intention or an accurate reflection of the significance of learner autonomy in the development of vocabulary use in writing. Coming to this topic last enables readers to reflect on the preceding chapters with a new lens, one that transfers the responsibility for learning vocabulary to the learner. **Learner autonomy**, then, describes a situation in which learners take responsibility for the goals and process of their learning and reflect on the success of the process as an evaluative exercise (Holec, 1981). Central to the concept of learner autonomy is the capacity for learners to take independent action based on critical reflection of their learning process (Little, 1991). This may require a new way of thinking about teaching and learning, in which the traditional roles of the teacher and learner are reshaped. Yeung (2019) talks of learner autonomy as a process of reducing learner reliance on the teacher. It may be a gradual process of learners assuming more control over their learning with the teacher still present and involved, rather than a complete transfer of all decisions from the teacher to the learner.

This chapter considers the ways that vocabulary learning can foster learner autonomy when it comes to writing.

Understanding Autonomous Learning

Learner autonomy can be described in several ways. First, we can talk of autonomous learners assuming an attitude toward learning that is full of self-discovery and self-reflection, representing an inward-looking process of exploration (Hyland, 2003). This signifies a learner's interest in the learning process and a strong intrinsic motivation to learn. This motivation is situated inside the learner and is represented by a personal commitment to the learning process, largely independent of the interest and encouragement conveyed by others.

Second, the autonomous learner assumes control over the learning objectives, the linguistic content, and the resources utilized in the learning process (Benson, 2013). This display of self-direction could continue through to the evaluative stage, in which the learner may take control over the focus and nature of feedback on performance.

Third, elements of autonomy are revealed when learners display a high level of strategic competence by adopting strategies that are suitable for the learning process, providing the learner with what Hirvela (2016) regards as a sense of control. Strategic learners have a broad range of approaches at their disposal and are aware of their significance and the possibilities for tailoring and combing these to maximize the scope for learning and performance.

Fostering Learner Independence

Learner autonomy has a key role to play in all aspects of acquiring a new language, but for writing instructors, because of the centrality of vocabulary in writing development and the need to tailor vocabulary learning to writer needs, it is particularly necessary to make autonomy part of the L2 writing classroom. It may not always be possible to monitor the degree of autonomy in our learners, but a clear measure of the benefit of learner autonomy is the extent to which it contributes to improved student performance in writing.

One particularly interesting dimension of learner autonomy is related to ownership of ideas, and how this is developed in writing. The thinking is that developing ownership requires the student to see their writing as a communicative act, with a clear purpose for a clear audience. In this regard, Morton and Storch (2019) take our attention to the notion of **authorial voice** in writing, reflecting on the nature of the relationship between writer and reader and how the writer shapes this through language (including vocabulary choice) and tone. Authorial voice is framed as writing that is "convincing, clear, engaging and conveying a sense of ownership" (p. 19). Morton and Storch see this quality of writing as particularly challenging for all students, with much of the research attention on authorial voice focused on the writing of doctoral students.

Creating opportunities to develop students' vocabulary learning autonomy gives room for them to shape the learning process to suit their specific needs, attitudes to learning, and preferences about vocabulary use. In the case of bilingual or multilingual writers, they will need to figure out what can and cannot be transferred from the L1 or from other languages they know. In indigenous languages, local experts (i.e., elders) in the community can provide a stepping-stone for the students to develop vocabulary knowledge in English that enables them to represent ideas from their home culture, reflecting an appreciation of linguistic diversity, as discussed in Hirsh (2013). Recognizing the social importance of home languages and culture in identity development and the effect of this on learning opens doors to new discussions and pedagogies that engage with and embrace community languages.

The value of fostering learner autonomy in relation to vocabulary use in writing is seen largely in the way this shapes the learner attitude to and experience of the writing process. It fits well with current ideas about self-directed learning as a powerful mechanism in human development (see Ryan & Deci, 2017) and also fits well with task-induced involvement (see Chapter 5) where opportunities to involve the learner deeply in the process of vocabulary learning and use enhance the opportunities for learning and retention to allow for production of newly acquired words in writing.

All writing is socially situated, in that it occurs within a particular social setting; therefore, we need to consider how appropriate learner autonomy would be to particular views held of learning and teaching and views held on the role of teacher and learner. Intraboonsom, Darasawang, and Reinders (2020) reflect on attempts to introduce ideas about learner autonomy in teacher-centered classroom environments where learners have been conditioned to behave in "passive and obedient" ways and where teachers are modeled as transmitters of knowledge. In such situations, teachers may find that their attempts to introduce learner autonomy can fail because they cannot reshape traditional roles in the classroom. In such cases, attitudes toward teaching and learning may need to change before learner autonomy can take hold.

What Should Teachers Do?

Teachers play an important role in encouraging independence in vocabulary learning. Lai, Yeung, and Hu (2016) describe teachers as "significant social agents who shape students' intellectual and social experiences" in the context of autonomous language learning (p. 703). Teachers are central to the decision to introduce autonomy into the L2 writing classroom at the institutional level, as the focus of action research or as a pedagogical initiative. Teachers also need to be encouraging about the value of autonomous learning. Teachers can model autonomous learning behaviors with students and train them using the tools that are available (see Chapter 7). As previously noted, some students may struggle with the concept of the teacher asking learners to lead their own learning, instead of formal instruction (Lai, Yeung, & Hu, 2016).

Beyond individual writing tasks, writing instructors can involve their learners in **collaborative writing** (Storch, 2005) with a focus on learner negotiation of meaning and language, shaped by learner needs and goals.

Teachers are responsible for evaluation and assessment so they do need to provide feedback and guide students regarding word choice, as well as ensuring the student's writing meets the goals of the task. In disciplinary writing, this includes the use of academic and technical terms, use of conjunctions, formation of claims, and use of hedging (Hyland, 1994) as well as the overall tone of the writing.

Teachers need to enable students to present themselves in writing in a way that reflects the nature of the writer-reader relationship and the goals of the task. For example, if students are writing to persuade, the teacher can lead students to reflect on how specific types of language use (and vocabulary) suits this type of writing. If students are writing to demonstrate their understanding of something and hope to open the eyes of their readers, teachers can comment on how the specific types of language help in this regard. To illustrate this point, students could be guided to reflect on the choice of verbs when reporting research, as with *Current research (proves/suggests),* where the verbs alter the strength of claims made. Where research in the field is ongoing and tentative in nature, *suggests* would come across as more suitable than *proves*, to allow for new possibilities and findings in the future (Kim & Lim, 2015). In these ways, providing feedback as students take the lead in their vocabulary learning is shaped by student performance, the nature of the writing, and the specific goals of the learner.

Some teachers may see the transition to autonomous modes as a diminishing of their role, in which their control over the students is eroded, potentially opening the door to disorganization, chaos, or a challenge to order. Behind such concerns and fears could be an awareness of the role of power in the L2 classroom and how it affects teacher-student dialogue and interaction. The transition can be particularly challenging for teachers who are used to teacher-centered classrooms (Tütüniş, 2011).

Nevertheless, research supports the student-centered classroom (Reinders & Balçikanli, 2011). Many settings provide practicing teachers with opportunities to observe autonomous learning in other classrooms to help them construct an image of themselves. In the end, there may be some settings in which autonomous learning is impeded because some students still expect that the teacher will assume and maintain control over the learning process. There may be a mismatch between bottom-up (i.e., localized) views on autonomous learning in a classroom, school, or community, and top-down (i.e., national) policies or directions on this concept, as conveyed at state or ministry levels.

Approaches to Independent Learning of Vocabulary

A popular way to encourage autonomous learning of vocabulary is through the use of **vocabulary cards** (sometimes referred to as flashcards). The basic ideas is that students write the target word on one side of the card and its translation in the L1 on the other (Nation & Webb, 2011). A picture could be used in place of the translation for concrete nouns such as *shoes, cat*, and *house*. Other models used with older or more advanced learners could see the target word on one side and information about the word (i.e., meaning, part of speech, collocation, example sentence) on the other side. An example word card for the word *domestic* appears in Figure 8.1.

Figure 8.1: Word Card for *domestic*

domestic	**Family:** *domestic (adj), domesticate (v), domestication (n), domesticated (adj)* **Meaning:** *within a country or house* **Collocations:** *domestic worker, domestic trade, domestic dispute* **Use:** *The airline provides more than 200 domestic flights daily.*

Source: Adapted from Paltridge et al., 2009, p. 99.

In an autonomous mode, young learners should develop word cards for vocabulary items they wish to use and/or are struggling with. Then they share their cards with other students and test each other to provide the target word when prompted by a picture or translation. Wilkinson (2017) utilized word cards with Japanese learners of English, in which students were instructed to enter information about selected words as L1 meaning, L2 form, and example sentence in the L2. Student comments on use of the bilingual word cards reveal the benefit; some are shown in Figure 8.2.

Figure 8.2: Student Comments on Use of Bilingual Word Cards

- Word cards are good, I think, good, good for me. I like this system very much ... I can learn many words quickly. ... I can choose words I don't know, it is good.
- It is good to learn new words and sentences, easy, quickly study many word. ... I can learn many words quickly, ... it is also convenient.
- Cards are a good way to study quickly. I can learn word and sentence well. ... I can know many new words and the way of using. ... English words and sentences.
- I have to see one side and remember the other, it is difficult but good for me. ... I can remember more easy next time. I see Japanese and have to remember word and sentence, is good.
- When I see Japanese word, I have to remember the English one, is difficult but helpful for me. ... If I see together, like notebook, maybe I do not remember next time.
- I like this, must think hard ... not easy ... cannot see both sides at same time, is good. Remembering sentence is good.
- I have to think about, remember the word on the other side of the card, it is good. I remember words like this more. In textbook, words shown together, it is too easy ... don't have to think.
- Sometimes I only bring some cards, not all of them. ... If I know some words I can leave them at home for that day's study.
- I will study from them again at next, or next session, because, if I finish with them, I think I forget them again. So, um, if I study them today and know them, or um get good test score, maybe I not study for one week.

Source: Wilkinson, 2017, pp. 6–7. Used with permission.

When it comes to the writing class, an alternative to cards is a vocabulary notebook, or **vocabulary logs.** Here, information about a vocabulary item is provided on different aspects including meaning, translation in the L1, parts of speech, pronunciation, collocations, antonyms, synonyms, as well as pictures and examples of the words in sentences. These learner-created resources engage learners deeply with the process of constructing entries for select words, representing a strong form of learner engagement, or task-induced involvement. An example of a vocabulary log with an entry completed for the word *succeed* appears in Figure 8.3.

Fowle (2002) describes how vocabulary notebooks (see also Folse, 2020) promoted autonomous vocabulary learning in a Thai secondary school setting. One of the guiding objectives was to encourage students to become more independent of the teacher. The teachers involved in the study introduced vocabulary notebooks to their learners as A–Z dictionaries in which students entered information on new vocabulary items that would assist them with effectively using newly acquired words. Students had control over the words to be included and the information entered, although teachers modeled examples of target words with information provided. A section of the notebooks was allocated for word families and representations of lexical relations (e.g., mind maps). Students could utilize their vocabulary notebook when writing to activate previously acquired words with a degree of confidence. Student experiences were overwhelmingly

Figure 8.3: Sample Vocabulary Log with Entry for *succeed*

New Word	Word Forms	Meaning	Use
succeed (v)	success (n) successful (adj) successfully (adv) unsuccessful (adj)	"to achieve what you planned or hoped"	*I will succeed in finding a job.*

positive, represented by comments such as these (Fowle, 2002: 386):

- It helps me understand nouns, adjectives, ...
- It helps us know the meaning of words.
- I can collect new words.
- It helps me remember difficult words.
- When I want to know the meaning of words, I'll use my vocabulary book.
- I can look in it when I forget words.
- It makes me more diligent.

Some comments made by teachers on the extent to which learner notebooks helped foster learner autonomy (Fowle, 2002: 386) are shown:

- Definitely. When they hear a new word they record it, and they refer to their books to remind them of the new language they have learnt.
- Not as much as hoped. My students still need direction.
- It does develop learner autonomy...most of my students automatically record words.

A Role for Translanguaging and the L1

One consideration with encouraging autonomy with multilingual students is the linguistic repertoire students bring to their writing and attitudes regarding using multiple languages simultaneously in the L2 writing classroom. This is informed by current thinking in bilingual and multilingual education contexts about translanguaging, captured in the words of Hornberger (2005: 607):

> Bi/multilinguals' learning is maximized when they are allowed and enabled to draw from across all their existing language skills (in two+ languages), rather than being constrained and inhibited from doing so by monolingual instructional assumptions and practices.

To illustrate the concept, consider a bilingual writing teacher with a group of L2 students who share an L1 and a mode of learning where the teacher and students weave in and out of the L1 naturally as they wish and need as a linguistic resource to assist with L2 writing development. The teacher can use the L1 to provide a word or a definition, convey a complex idea, or present a humorous anecdote from the teacher's past. In a dual-language program with equal numbers of students from the two language backgrounds being taught (e.g., Spanish and English), students could be paired with one dominant in each language to promote translanguaging and create mini master-apprentice learning situations, facilitating shared construction of stories in both languages.

Instances of translanguaging are evident in the spoken language production of Arabic learners of English shown, with Arabic words underlined and English translations provided in square brackets (Kniaź, 2017: 204–205):

- ana [I] my school was expensive
- btūʿ il-handasa [those in engineering] they used to speak more Arabic
- bass ana ahli masalan [but I my family for example], they don't pray as much
- and now il-banāt [the girls] are the majority

One issue facing L2 writing teachers is how to respond to ideas about discovering the languages of their learners and opening the door for conversations in the classroom about the role of L1 vocabulary knowledge in L2 writing. This process would require a substantive change of thinking for those trained under a doctrine of creating distinct separation of languages in the writing class where use of the L1 is seen as an impediment to L2 learning and is discouraged in the L2 classroom. It may also require a fully bilingual teacher with a homogenous (i.e., shared L1) group of L2 learners to ensure the teacher has literacy dominance over the students in both the L1 and L2 and, thus, can maintain a teacher role when both languages are in use.

New ideas about use of languages in the classroom are relevant for learners with a well-developed L1 literacy but limited L2 vocabulary knowledge who may benefit from use of L1 vocabulary items as a stepping stone to introducing the L2 equivalent in their writing. Within a framework of translanguaging, multilingual students are encouraged to draw on their full linguistic repertoire for communication. García (2013) sees translanguaging as a positive and important development for language-minority students, enhancing the status of "minority" languages in the L2 classroom alongside "dominant" languages. Velasco and García (2014), among others, report on translanguaging practice being used in the context of K–4 writing with students speaking Spanish-to-English and Korean-to-English in a New York City school with positive effect.

From an L2 vocabulary perspective, the advice given to students could be to enter an L1 word where this would facilitate continuity of ideas development within the L2 composition. The idea would be for the students to change this to the L2 form in a subsequent draft, representing a meaningful process of vocabulary development.

Turnbull (2017) encourages a new approach to assessment tasks for multilingual learners that would be suited to dual-language programs that seek to foster literacy in more than one language. This approach would embrace the learner's home language experiences to provide a more valid means of assessing language use in a bilingual setting. A writing task, for example, could require a version in the L1 and a version in the L2. Such an approach could be well suited to primary school settings where assessment tasks are typically low-stakes and designed to promote learning.

The field is still at a relatively early stage regarding translanguaging into the L2 writing classroom, but, as Ortega (2013) reminds us, there is a bilingual turn taking hold in ESL and EFL classrooms in which bilingual and multilingual learners are understood in terms of the linguistic repertoire they bring with them into the classroom, which will see new ideas emerge and take hold. It will be critical for L2 teacher training programs to emphasize the need to view bilingual and multilingual students in terms of the languages they know and can use and to consider how the L2 writing classroom is an environment that can break down traditional barriers between languages and open up a space where all languages are valued, without prejudice or judgment. The L2 writing classroom promotes positive student identities with their L1s, which encourages multilingualism, multiliteracy practices, and plurilingual values in all domains of life.

Key Points

1. In seeking to introduce or enhance learner autonomy in the L2 writing class regarding vocabulary use, teachers need to be cognizant of the values, beliefs, and practices of the learners and the wider society they identify with.
2. Learner differences greatly affect independence in writing. In a teacher-centered class, some learners may exhibit a high degree of independence, albeit constrained by the behavior of the teacher and other students. In an independent learning program, some students may exhibit a reliance on others, particularly support staff and teachers. Thus, calling an approach "independent" does not guarantee independent learner behavior.
3. Learners may need guidance, training, and modeling of effective modes of independent behavior. If an independent vocabulary learning log is used, learners may benefit from seeing one from a previous student cohort. If learners are encouraged to explore word collocations in a corpus through generation of concordance lines, they will require substantial support with various steps along the way. Where such programs are offered as optional classes for doctoral students, attrition is noted, suggesting that this approach is not for everyone.
4. Teachers will vary in their attitude toward fostering independence in their learners, and this may reflect ideas about their role in the classroom, the type of relationship they seek to develop with their students, and their previous experience with learner independence. Staff workshops can identify any concerns and consider appropriate ways to accommodate these. In the end, teachers cannot be effectively forced to implement independence in their learners; an effective implementation requires strong teacher commitment and a willingness to invest time and effort.

Sample Activities for the Classroom

Activity 1: Elementary School Level

In a dual-language elementary school writing classroom, the teacher has invited a local elder to be part of a writing project during several class sessions in which students are tasked with writing a story in two languages, first in the L1 and then in the L2, based on their home culture. They are encouraged to illustrate the story. The local elder will provide knowledge and linguistic resource to assist with development of L1 stories. A core component of the process is a shared vocabulary board in the classroom where students add vocabulary items in the L1 and L2 that are included in their stories. These words become a central focus for developing their ideas. The teacher then asks the students to share their completed stories with their classmates, reading the stories aloud first in the L1 and then in the L2. The completed stories are turned into big books and used as a learning resource in the school for current and future students.

Activity 2: High School Level

A high school class includes L2 students from a range of language backgrounds and with variable levels of English proficiency. The teacher shares with the class ideas about translanguaging as a positive development in multilingual classrooms. In a writing task, the teacher invites bilingual and multilingual students in the class to introduce occasional words from the L1 (or L3) in cases where there is an idea they wish to convey in the L2 for which they lack knowledge of the correct L2 word. The teacher then encourages students to use these L1 and L3 lexical items as the focus for vocabulary development in the L2, resulting in a subsequent draft of the writing.

Activity 3: Graduate Level

L2 students from a wide range of academic disciplines in the university are enrolled in a graduate course titled Writing in Academic Settings. As part of the course requirements, they are to undertake a research project of 3,000 words titled "Context

Analysis." They are to analyze the nature of writing in their disciplinary area, including a focus on vocabulary use, through various means including analysis of expert writing in the field (i.e., vocabulary analysis of published writing), a lexical analysis of their own writing as a point of comparison with expert writing, an interview with an academic member of staff in their area on lecturer expectations of writing, and a personal reflection on their writing development as an undergraduate student. Sources from writing on the disciplinary nature of vocabulary use are to inform the discussion. Students are trained how to use online tools to analyze corpora and their own writing and are guided in adopting a reflective frame to encourage deep considerations of their changing perceptions and understandings. The teacher explains to the students that they are to gain an insider's view of their discourse community, adopting an ethnographic perspective, and that this will encourage their transition from novice to expert writers. They are encouraged to reflect on their changing assumptions about the nature of writing in their disciplinary area, particularly for students who moved into the university from a different academic setting in their undergraduate studies. The students work independently on their projects during the semester and report back to class toward the end of the course in the form of a seminar presentation in which they share their findings. The teacher notes a strong philosophical focus with reflective commentary in the better projects, suggesting a deep and insightful reflection of students aspiring to become part of a community of researchers.

Tasks and Discussion Questions for Teachers

1. *Learner autonomy* and *learner independence* are not new terms in language teaching. However, they are not always given strong attention by teachers. This means that students may, in some classrooms, be left to develop this aspect of their learning without guidance and support from the teacher. What are your own attitudes toward fostering learner independence in the L2 writing classroom?
2. How much independence do your L2 writing students currently have in terms of vocabulary learning and use in writing?
3. As a pilot program designed to support indigenous and minority language use in mainstream schools, writing tasks in your elementary school are re-designed to include a translanguaging dimension. Students are encouraged to bring their full linguistic repertoire to their writing. What might you expect to see in the writing of bilingual and multilingual students?

References

Ai, H. (2020). Web-based L2 syntactic complexity [Computer software]. Retrieved from https://aihaiyang.com/software/

Akbarian, I., Farajollahi, F., & Jiménez Catalán, R. M. (2020). EFL learners' lexical availability: Exploring frequency, exposure, and vocabulary level. *System, 91, 102261.*

Anthony, L. (2019). AntConc (Version 3.5.8) [Computer software]. Tokyo: Waseda University. Retrieved from https://www.laurenceanthony.net/software/antconc

Antle, J. B. (2018). *Collocations and action research: Learning vocabulary through collocations.* London: Bloomsbury Academic.

Ardasheva, Y., & Tretter, T. R. (2017). Developing science-specific, technical vocabulary of high school newcomer English learners. *International Journal of Bilingual Education and Bilingualism, 20*(3), 252–271.

Ash, M., Lofts, G., & Evergreen, M. J. (1998). *Jacaranda science 2.* Milton, Australia: John Wiley.

Astika, G. G. (1993). Analytical assessment of foreign student's writing. *RELC Journal, 24,* 61–72.

Baeskow, H. (2006). A revival of Romance roots. *Morphology, 16,* 3–36.

Barcroft, J. (2015). *Lexical input processing and vocabulary learning.* Amsterdam: John Benjamins.

Bauer, L., & Nation, P. (1993). Word families. *International Journal of Lexicography, 6*(4), 253–279.

Belcher, D. (2012). Considering what we know and need to know about second language writing. *Applied Linguistics Review, 3*(1), 131–150.

Benson, M., Benson, E., & Ilson, R. (Eds.). (1997). *The BBI dictionary of English word combinations.* Amsterdam: John Benjamins.

Benson, P. (2013). *Teaching and researching: Autonomy in language learning.* New York: Routledge.

Boers, F., & Webb, S. (2018). Teaching and learning collocation in adult second and foreign language learning. *Language Teaching, 51*(1), 77–89.

Boulton, A. (2017). Corpora in language teaching and learning. *Language Teaching, 50*(4), 483–506.

Brezina, V., & Gablasova, D. (2015). Is there a core general vocabulary? Introducing the new general service list. *Applied Linguistics, 36*(1), 1–22.

British National Corpus (BNC). (2007). *British National Corpus* (Version 3). Distributed by Bodleian Libraries, University of Oxford, on behalf of the BNC Consortium. Retrieved from http://www.natcorp.ox.ac.uk

Browne, C. (2014). A new general service list: The better mousetrap we've been looking for? *Vocabulary Learning and Instruction, 3*(2), 1–10.

Campion, M., & Elley, W. (1971). *An academic vocabulary list.* Wellington: New Zealand Council for Educational Research.

Carrió-Pastor, M., & Mestre-Mestre, E. (2014). Lexical errors in second language scientific writing: Some conceptual implications. *International Journal of English Studies, 14*(1), 97–108.

Centre for English Corpus Linguistics (2020). *Learner corpora around the world.* Louvain-la-Neuve, Belgium: Université Catholique de Louvain. Retrieved from https://uclouvain.be/en/research-institutes/ilc/cecl/learner-corpora-around-the-world.html

Chen, A. (2019). Assessing phraseological development in word sequences of variable lengths in second language texts using directional association measures. *Language Learning, 69*(2), 440–477.

Chen, M., & Flowerdew, J. (2018). A critical review of research and practice in data-driven learning (DDL) in the academic writing classroom. *International Journal of Corpus Linguistics, 23*(3), 335–369.

Cho, S. (2017). Processing and learning of English collocations: An eye movement study. *Language Teaching Research, 21*(3), 403–426.

CLARIN. (2020). *L2 learner corpora.* Retrieved from https://www.clarin.eu/resource-families/L2-corpora

Cobb, T. (2020). *Compleat Lexical Tutor.* Retrieved from https://www.lextutor.ca

CoRD (2020). *Corpora finder.* Retrieved from http://www.helsinki.fi/varieng/CoRD/corpora/corpusfinder/

Corpus Linguistics. (2020). *DIY corpora: Building and using your own corpora.* Lancashire, England: Department of Linguistics and Modern English Language, University of Lancaster. Retrieved from https://www.lancaster.ac.uk/fss/courses/ling/corpus/blue/diy_top.htm

Coxhead, A. (2000). A new academic word list. *TESOL Quarterly, 34*(2), 213–238.

Coxhead, A. (2006). *Essentials of teaching academic vocabulary.* Boston: Houghton Mifflin.

Coxhead, A. (2007). Factors and aspects of knowledge affecting L2 word use in writing. In P. Davidson, C. Coombe, D. Lloyd, & D. Palfreyman (Eds.), *Teaching and learning vocabulary in another language* (pp. 331–342). Dubai: TESOL Arabia.

Coxhead, A., & Byrd, P. (2007). Preparing writing teachers to teach the vocabulary and grammar of academic prose. *Journal of Second Language Writing, 16*(3), 129–147.

Coxhead, A., & Hirsh, D. (2007). A pilot science-specific word list. *Revue Francaise de Linguistique Appliquee, 12*(2), 65–78.

Darus, S., & Subramaniam, K. (2009). Error analysis of the written English essays of secondary students in Malaysia: A case study. *European Journal of Social Sciences, 8*(3), 483–495.

Davies, M. (2008–2020). *The Corpus of Contemporary American English (COCA): One billion words, 199–219.* Retrieved from https://www.english-corpora.org/coca

Davies, M. (2013). Google Scholar and COCA-Academic: Two very different approaches to examining academic English. *Journal of English for Academic Purposes, 12*(3), 155–165.

de Jong, E. (2004). L2 proficiency development in a two-way and a developmental bilingual program. *NABE Journal of Research and Practice, 2*(1), 77–108.

Diaz, I. (2015). Training in metacognitive strategies for students' vocabulary improvement by using learning journals. *PROFILE Issues in Teachers' Professional Development, 17*(1), 87–102.

Durán, P., Malvern, D., Richards, B., & Chipere, N. (2004). Developmental trends in lexical diversity. *Applied Linguistics, 25*(2), 220–242.

Durrant, P. (2009). Investigating the viability of a collocation list for students of English for academic purposes. *English for Specific Purposes, 28*(3), 157–169.

Elley, W. B. (2000). The potential of book floods for raising literacy levels. *International Review of Education, 46*(3/4), 233–255.

Engber, C. (1993). The relationship of lexis to quality in L2 compositions. Paper delivered at TESOL Conference, Atlanta.

Erkaya, O. R. (2012). Vocabulary and L1 interference: Error analysis of Turkish students' English essays. *MEXTESOL Journal, 36*(2), 1–11.

Espinal, M. T., & Mateu, J. (2010). On classes of idioms and their interpretations. *Journal of Pragmatics, 42*, 1397–1411.

Ferris, D. R. (2011). *Treatment of error in second language student writing* (2nd ed.). Ann Arbor: University of Michigan Press.

Flint, P., Dollar, T., & Stewart, M. (2018). Building relationships with adolescent newcomers through literacy development. *Journal of Adolescent & Adult Literacy, 62*(5), 509–519.

Folse, K. (2010). Is explicit vocabulary focus the reading teacher's job? *Reading in a Foreign Language, 22*(1), 139–160.

Folse, K. (2020). *Teaching vocabulary is the writing teacher's job: Why and how.* Ann Arbor: University of Michigan Press.

Fowle, C. (2002). Vocabulary notebooks: Implementation and outcomes. *ELT Journal, 56*(4), 380–388.

Frankenberg-Garcia, A. (2012). Learners' use of corpus examples. *International Journal of Lexicography, 25*(3), 273–296.

García, O. (2013). Theorizing and enacting translanguaging for social justice. In A. Blackledge & A. Creese (Eds.), *Heteroglossia as practice and pedagogy* (pp. 199–216). New York: Springer.

Ghadessy, P. (1979). Frequency counts, word lists, and materials preparation: A new approach. *English Teaching Forum, 17*, 24–27.

Goulden, R., Nation, P., & Read, J. (1990). How large can a receptive vocabulary be? *Applied Linguistics, 11*(4), 341–363.

Graesser, A. C., McNamara, D. S., Louwerse, M. M., & Cai, Z. (2004). Coh-Metrix: Analysis of text on cohesion and language. *Behavior Research Methods, Instruments & Computers, 36*(2), 193–202.

Grami, G. (2020). An evaluation of online and automated English writing assistants: Collocations and idioms checkers. *International Journal of Emerging Technologies in Learning, 15*(4), 218–226.

Grant, L., & Ginther, A. (2000). Using computer-tagged linguistic features to describe L2 writing differences. *Journal of Second Language Writing, 9*(2), 123–145.

Greaves, C., & Warren, M. (2010). What can a corpus tell us about multi-word units? In A. O'Keeffe & M. McCarthy (Eds.), *The Routledge handbook of corpus linguistics* (pp. 212–226). London: Routledge.

Green, C., & Lambert, J. (2018). Advancing disciplinary literacy through English for academic purposes: Discipline-specific wordlists, collocations and word families for eight secondary subjects. *Journal of English for Academic Purposes, 35*, 105–115.

Guo, L., Crossley, S. A., & McNamara, D. S. (2013). Predicting human judgments of essay quality in both integrated and independent second language writing samples: A comparison study. *Assessing Writing, 18*(3), 218–238.

Haastrup, K., & Henriksen, B. (2000). Vocabulary acquisition: Acquiring depth of knowledge through network building. *International Journal of Applied Linguistics, 10*(2), 221–240.

Harklau, L., Losey, K., & Siegal, M. (Eds.). (1999). *Generation 1.5 meets college composition: Issues in the teaching of writing to U.S.-educated learners of ESL.* Mahwah, NJ: Lawrence Erlbaum.

Hashimoto, B., & Egbert, J. (2019). More than frequency? Exploring predictors of word difficulty for second language learners. *Language Learning, 69*(4), 839–872.

Hayes, J. (2012). Modeling and remodeling writing. *Written Communication, 29*(3), 369–388.

Hayes, J., & Flower, L. (1980). Identifying the organization of writing processes. In L. Gregg & E. Steinberg (Eds.), *Cognitive processes in writing* (pp. 3–30). Hillsdale, NJ: Lawrence Erlbaum.

Heatley, A., Nation, I. S. P., & Coxhead, A. (2002). *Range and frequency programs* [Computer software]. Retrieved from http://www.victoria.ac.nz/lals/staff/paul-nation.aspx

Hemchua, S., & Schmitt, N. (2006). An analysis of lexical errors in the English compositions of Thai learners. *Prospect, 21*(3), 3–25.

Henriksen, B. (1999). Three dimensions of vocabulary development. *Studies in Second Language Acquisition, 21*(2), 303–317.

Henriksen, B., & Haastrup, K. (1998). Vocabulary acquisition: From partial to precise understanding. In *K. Haastrup* & Å. Viberg (Eds.), *Perspectives on lexical acquisition in a second language* (pp. 97–124). Lund, Sweden: Lund University Press.

Hill, J., & Morgan, M. (1997). *LTP dictionary of selected collocations.* Boston: Cengage.

Hirsh, D. (2013). *Endangered languages, knowledge systems and belief systems.* Bern, Switzerland: Peter Lang.

Hirsh, D., & Nation, I. S. P. (1992). What vocabulary size is needed to read unsimplified texts for pleasure? *Reading in a Foreign Language, 8*(2), 689–696.

Hirvela, A. (2016). *Connecting reading and writing in second language writing instruction* (2nd ed.). Ann Arbor: University of Michigan Press.

Holec, H. (1981). *Autonomy and foreign language learning.* Oxford: Pergamon Press.

Hornberger, N. H. (2005). Opening and filling up implementational and ideological spaces in heritage language education. *Modern Language Journal, 89*, 605–609.

Horst, M., Cobb, T., & Meara, P. (1998). Beyond a clockwork orange: Acquiring second language vocabulary through reading. *Reading in a Foreign Language, 11*, 207–223.

Huang, C. Y., Huang, Y. T., Chen, M. H., & Ku, L. W. (2019). From receptive to productive: Learning to use confusing words through automatically selected example sentences. *The 14th Workshop on Innovative Use of NLP for Building Educational Applications* (pp. 461–471), Florence, Italy.

Huang, P., & Tsao, N. (2019). Using collocation clusters to detect and correct English L2 learners' collocation errors. *Computer Assisted Language Learning*, 1–27.

Huang, P., & Tsao, N. (2020). *NetCollo 2.0.* Retrieved from http://www.netcollo.info

Hwang, K., & Nation, I. S. P. (1989). Reducing the vocabulary load and encouraging vocabulary learning through reading newspapers. *Reading in a Foreign Language, 6*, 323–335.

Hyland, K. (1994). Hedging in academic textbooks and EAP. *English for Specific Purposes, 13*, 239–256.

Hyland, K. (2003). Genre-based pedagogies: A social response to process. *Journal of Second Language Writing, 12*(1), 17–29.

Hyland, K. (2008). As can be seen: Lexical bundles and disciplinary variation. *English for Specific Purposes, 27*(1), 4–21.

Hyland, K., & Tse, P. (2007). Is there an "academic vocabulary"? *TESOL Quarterly, 41*(2), 235–253.

Intraboonsom, C., Darasawang, P., & Reinders, H. (2020). Teachers' practices in fostering learner autonomy in a Thai university context. *Journal of Language Teaching and Research, 11*(2), 194–203.

Jarvis, S. (2013). Capturing the diversity in lexical diversity. *Language Learning, 63*(1), 87–106.

Johns, A. M. (1997). *Text, role, and context: Developing academic literacies.* Cambridge, England: Cambridge University Press.

Johnson, M., Acevedo, A., & Mercado, L. (2016). Vocabulary knowledge and vocabulary use in second language writing. *TESOL Journal, 7*(3), 700–771.

Kim, L., & Lim, J. (2015). Hedging in academic writing: A pedagogically-motivated study. *Procedia Social and Behavioral Sciences, 197*, 600–607.

Kırkgöz, Y. (2010). An analysis of written errors of Turkish adult learners of English. *Procedia Social and Behavioral Sciences, 2*, 4352–4358.

Kniaź, M. (2017). English lexical items in Egyptian Arabic. Code-switching or borrowing? *Alicante Journal of English Studies, 30*, 185–210.

Krashen, S. (1989). We acquire vocabulary and spelling by reading: Additional evidence for the Input Hypothesis. *Modern Language Journal, 73*(4), 440–464.

Kumaravadivelu, B. (2006). *Understanding language teaching: From method to postmethod.* London: Routledge.

Kyle, K., Crossley, S. A., & Berger, C. (2018). The tool for the automatic analysis of lexical sophistication (TAALES): Version 2.0. *Behavior Research Methods, 50*, 1030–1046.

Lai, C., Yeung, Y., & Hu, J. (2016). University student and teacher perceptions of teacher roles in promoting autonomous language learning with technology outside the classroom. *Computer Assisted Language Learning, 29*(4), 703–723.

Laufer, B. (1988). The concept of "synforms" (similar lexical forms) in L2 vocabulary acquisition. *Language and Education, 2*, 113–132.

Laufer, B. (1989). A factor of difficulty in vocabulary learning: Deceptive transparency. *AILA Review, 6*(1), 10–20.

Laufer, B. (1998). The development of passive and active vocabulary in a second language: Same or different? *Applied Linguistics, 19*, 255–271.

Laufer, B., & Hulstijn, J. H. (2001). Incidental vocabulary acquisition in a second language: The construct of task-induced involvement. *Applied Linguistics, 22*, 1–26.

Laufer, B., & Nation, I. S. P. (1995). Vocabulary size and use: Lexical richness in L2 written production. *Applied Linguistics, 16*(3), 307–322.

Laufer, B., & Nation, I. S. P. (1999). A vocabulary-size test of controlled productive ability. *Language Testing, 16*(1), 36–55.

Laufer, B., & Waldman, T. (2011). Verb-noun collocations in second language writing: A corpus analysis of learners' English. *Language Learning, 61*(2), 647–672.

Lee, D., & Swales, J. (2006). A corpus-based EAP course for NNS doctoral students: Moving from available specialized corpora to self-compiled corpora. *English for Specific Purposes, 25*(1), 56–75.

Lee, S. H. (2003). ESL learners' vocabulary use in writing and the effects of explicit vocabulary instruction. *System, 31*(4), 537–561.

Leech, G. (2011). Frequency, corpora and language learning. In F. Meunier, S. de Cock, G. Gilquin, & M. Paquot (Eds), *A taste for corpora* (pp. 7–31). Amsterdam: John Benjamins.

Lei, L., & Liu, D. (2016). A new medical academic word list: A corpus-based study with enhanced methodology. *Journal of English for Academic Purposes, 22*, 42–53.

Little, D. (1991). *Learner autonomy: Definitions, issues and problems.* Dublin: Authentik.

Lynn, R. (1973). Preparing word lists: A suggested method. *RELC Journal, 4*(1), 25–32.

Ma, J., & Cheon, H. (2018). An experimental study of dictionary use on vocabulary learning and reading comprehension in different task conditions. *International Journal of Lexicography, 31*(1), 29–52.

Malvern, D., & Richards, B. (2002). Investigating accommodation in language proficiency interviews using a new measure of lexical diversity. *Language Testing, 19*(1), 85–104.

Matsuoka, W., & Hirsh, D. (2010). Vocabulary learning through reading: Does an ELT course book provide good opportunities? *Reading in a Foreign Language, 22*(1), 56–70.

Matsuoka, W., & Hirsh, D. (2018). The specialised vocabulary of high school science. In D. Hirsh (Ed.), *Explorations in second language vocabulary research* (pp. 51–99). Bern, Switzerland: Peter Lang.

McCarthy, P. M., & Jarvis, S. (2010). MTLD, vocd-D, and HD-D: A validation study of sophisticated approaches to lexical diversity assessment. *Behavior Research Methods, 42*, 381–392.

Meara, P. (1998). Review of second language vocabulary acquisition: A rationale for pedagogy. *Applied Linguistics, 19*(2), 289–292.

Meara, P., & Alcoy, J. (2010). Words as species: An alternative approach to estimating productive vocabulary size. *Reading in a Foreign Language, 22*(1), 222–236.

Meara, P., & Bell, H. (2001). P_Lex: A simple and effective way of describing the lexical characteristics of short L2 texts. *Prospect, 16*(3), 5–19.

MICUSP. (2009). Michigan Corpus of Upper-level Student Papers. Ann Arbor: The Regents of the University of Michigan. Retrieved from http://micusp.elicorpora.info

Milton, J. (2013). Measuring the contribution of vocabulary knowledge to proficiency in the four skills. In C. Bardel, C. Lindqvist, & B. Laufer (Eds.), *L2 vocabulary acquisition, knowledge and use: New perspectives on assessment and corpus analysis* (pp. 57–78). Eurosla Monographs Series, 2, Amsterdam: Eurosla.

Milton, J., Wade, J., & Hopkins, N. (2010). Aural word recognition and oral competence in a foreign language. In R. Chacón-Beltrán, C. Abello-Contesse, & M. Torreblanca-López (Eds.), *Insights into non-native vocabulary teaching and learning* (pp. 83–98). Bristol, England: Multilingual Matters.

Miralpeix, I., & Muñoz, C. (2018). Receptive vocabulary size and its relationship to EFL language skills. *International Review of Applied Linguistics in Language Teaching, 56*(1), 1–24.

Mochizuki, M., & Aizawa, K. (2000). An affix acquisition order for EFL learners, an exploratory study. *System, 28*(2), 291–304.

Morton, J., & Storch, N. (2019). Developing an authorial voice in PhD multilingual student writing: The reader's perspective. *Journal of Second Language Writing, 43,* 15–23.

Nation, I. S. P. (1983). Testing and teaching vocabulary. *Guidelines, 5*(1), 12–25.

Nation, I. S. P. (2001). *Learning vocabulary in another language.* Cambridge, England: Cambridge University Press.

Nation, I. S. P. (2015). Principles guiding vocabulary learning through extensive reading. *Reading in a Foreign Language, 27*(1), 136–145.

Nation, I. S. P., & Gu, P. Y. (2007). *Focus on vocabulary.* Sydney: National Centre for English Language Teaching and Research.

Nation, I. S. P., & Webb, S. (2011). *Researching and analyzing vocabulary.* Boston: Heinle/Cengage.

Nation, I. S. P., & Yamamoto, A. (2012). Applying the four strands to language learning. *International Journal of Innovation in English Language Teaching and Research, 1*(2), 173–187.

Nelson, G. (2016–2020). *International Corpus of English* [Corpus data set]. Retrieved from http://ice-corpora.net/ice

Nesselhauf, N. (2005). *Collocations in a learner corpus.* Amsterdam: John Benjamins.

O'Donnell, M. (2019). UAM Computer Tools (Version 3.3v2) [Computer software]. Madrid: Universidad Autónoma de Madrid. Retrieved from http://www.corpustool.com

Ok, S. (2014). Reflections of ELT students on their progress in language and vocabulary use in portfolio process. *English Language Teaching, 7*(2), 53–62.

Ortega, L. (2013). SLA for the 21st century: Disciplinary progress, transdisciplinary relevance, and the bi/multilingual turn. *Language Learning, 63*(1), 1–24.

Otto, P. (2021). Choosing specialized vocabulary to teach with data-driven learning: An example from civil engineering. *English for Specific Purposes, 61,* 32–46.

Otwinowska, A., & Szewczyk, J. (2019). The more similar the better? Factors in learning cognates, false cognates and non-cognate words. *International Journal of Bilingual Education and Bilingualism, 22*(8), 974–991.

Paltridge, B., Harbon, L., Hirsh, D., Shen, H., Stevenson, M., Phakiti, A., & Woodrow, L. (2009). *Teaching academic writing: An introduction for teachers of second language writers.* Ann Arbor: University of Michigan Press.

Paribakht, T., & Wesche, M. (1997). Vocabulary enhancement activities and reading for meaning in second language acquisition. In J. Coady & T. Huckin (Eds), *Second language vocabulary acquisition* (pp. 174–200). Cambridge, England: Cambridge University Press.

Park, T., Lank, E., Poupart, P., & Terry, M. (2008). Is the sky pure today? AwkChecker: An assistive tool for detecting and correcting collocation errors. *Proceedings of the 21st Annual ACM Symposium on User Interface Software and Technology* (pp. 121–130). Monterey, CA: ACM Press.

Praninskas, J. (1972). *American university word list.* London: Longman.

Raimes, A. (1983). *Techniques in teaching writing.* New York: Oxford University Press.

Rasinski, T., Padak, N., Newton, J., & Newton, E. (2011). The Latin-Greek connection: Building vocabulary through morphological study. *The Reading Teacher, 65*(2), 133–141.

Rassaei, E. (2012). The effects of input-based and output-based instruction on L2 development. *The Electronic Journal for English as a Second Language, 16*(3), 1–25.

Rauser, D. (2017). Selected English-Czech false friends and their use in the works of some Czech students. *Caracteres (Salamanca),* 6(1), 209–237.

Read, J. (1993). The development of a new measure of L2 vocabulary knowledge. *Language Testing, 10*(3), 355–371.

Read, J. (1998). Validating a test to measure depth of vocabulary knowledge. In A. J. Kunnan (Ed.), *Validation in language assessment* (pp. 41–60). Mahwah, NJ: Lawrence Erlbaum.

Reinders, H., & Balcikanli, C. (2011). Learning to foster autonomy: The role of teacher education materials. *Studies in Self-Access Learning Journal, 2*(1), 15–25.

Reppen, R. (2010). Building a corpus. In A. O'Keeffe & M. McCarthy (Eds.), *The Routledge handbook of corpus linguistics* (pp. 31–38). London: Routledge.

Richards, J. (1976). The role of vocabulary teaching. *TESOL Quarterly, 10*(1), 77–89.

Römer, U. (2008). Corpora and language teaching. In A. Lüdeling & M. Kyto (Eds.), *Corpus linguistics: An international handbook* (Vol. 1, pp. 112–130). Berlin: Mouton de Gruyter.

Ryan, R. M., & Deci, E. L. (2017). *Self-determination: Basic psychological needs in motivation, development, and wellness.* New York: Guilford Press.

Salazar, D. (2014). *Lexical bundles in native and non-native scientific writing: Applying a corpus-based study to language teaching.* Amsterdam: John Benjamins.

Schmidt, R. (1990). The role of consciousness in second language learning. *Applied Linguistics, 11*(2), 129–158.

Schmidt, R. (1994). Implicit learning and the cognitive unconscious: Of artificial grammars and SLA. In N. Ellis (Ed.), *Implicit and explicit learning of languages* (pp. 165–209). London: Academic Press.

Schmitt, N., Schmitt, D., & Clapham, C. (2001). Developing and exploring the behaviour of two new versions of the Vocabulary Levels Test. *Language Testing, 18*(1), 55–88.

Schoonen, R., van Gelderen, A., Stoel, R., Hulstijn, J., & de Glopper, K. (2011). Modeling the development of L1 and EFL writing proficiency of secondary school students. *Language Learning, 61*(1), 31–79.

Scott, M. (2020). *WordSmith Tools* (Version 8). Stroud: Lexical analysis software. Retrieved from https://www.lexically.net/wordsmith

Selinker, L. (1972). Interlanguage. *International Review of Applied Linguistics, 10*(3), 209–232.

Shi, B., Huang, L., & Lu, X. (2020). Effect of prompt type on test-takers' writing performance and writing strategy use in the continuation task. *Language Testing, 37*(3), 361–388.

Shimron, J. (2003). Semitic languages: Are they really root-based? In J. Shimron (Ed.), *Language processing and acquisition in languages of Semitic, root-based, morphology* (pp. 1–28). Amsterdam: John Benjamins.

Shirzad, M., Rasekh, A. E., & Dabaghi, A. (2017). The effects of input and output tasks on the learning and retention of EAP vocabulary. *Theory and Practice in Language Studies, 7*(2), 145–152.

Sketch Engine (2020). *Create a corpus from the Web.* Retrieved from https://www.sketchengine.eu/guide/create-a-corpus-from-the-web

Spolsky, B. (2007). Language policy. *International Journal of Applied Linguistics, 17*(2), 268–270.

Stæhr, L. S. (2008). Vocabulary size and the skills of listening, reading and writing, *Language Learning Journal, 36*(2), 139–152.

St. John, M., & Dudley-Evans, T. (1998). *Developments in English for specific purposes.* Cambridge, England: Cambridge University Press.

Storch, N. (2005). Collaborative writing: Product, process, and students' reflections. *Journal of Second Language Writing, 14*(3), 153–173.

Swales, J. (1990). *Genre analysis: English in academic and research settings.* Cambridge, England: Cambridge University Press.

Turnbull, B. (2017). Towards new standards in foreign language assessment: Learning from bilingual education. *International Journal of Bilingual Education and Bilingualism,* 1–11.

Tütüniş, B. (2011). Changing teacher beliefs and attitudes towards autonomous learning. In D. Gardner (Ed.), *Fostering autonomy in language learning* (pp. 161–165). Gaziantep, Turkey: Zirve University.

University of Sydney (2007). *ENGG1800 Practical Manual*. Faculty of Engineering.

Varnaseri, M. (2016). The relationship between depth and breadth vocabulary knowledge and writing performance of Iranian MA students of TEFL. *Modern Journal of Language Teaching Methods, 6*(2), 544–554.

Velasco, P., & García, O. (2014). Translanguaging and the writing of bilingual learners. *Bilingual Research Journal, 37*(1), 6–23.

Vögelin, C., Jansen, T., Keller, S., Machts, N., & Möller, J. (2019). The influence of lexical features on teacher judgements of ESL argumentative essays. *Assessing Writing, 39*, 50–63.

Wang, J-H. T. (2015). Task-induced involvement load: The accumulation effects on vocabulary acquisition. *Chinese Journal of Applied Linguistics, 38*(2), 150–165.

Ward, J. (2009). A basic engineering English word list for less proficient foundation engineering undergraduates. *English for Specific Purposes, 28*(3), 170–182.

Webb, S. (2007). The effects of repetition on vocabulary knowledge. *Applied Linguistics, 28*, 46–65.

Weisser, M. (2020). *Specialised corpora*. Retrieved from http://martinweisser.org/corpora_site/spec_corpora.html

Wesche, M., & Paribakht, T. (1996). Assessing second language vocabulary knowledge: Depth versus breadth. *Canadian Modern Language Review, 53*(1), 13–40.

West, M. (1953). *A general service list of English words*. London: Longman, Green & Co.

Wilkinson, D. (2017). EFL vocabulary acquisition through word cards: Student perceptions and strategies. *TESL-EJ, 21*(3), 1–16.

Xu, Y., & Wu, Z. (2012). Test-taking strategies for a high-stakes writing test: an exploratory study of 12 Chinese EFL learners. *Assessing Writing, 17*(3), 174–190.

Yang, M. (2015). A nursing academic word list. *English for Specific Purposes, 37*(1), 27–38.

Yeung, M. (2019). Exploring the strength of the process writing approach as a pedagogy for fostering learner autonomy in writing among young learners. *English Language Teaching, 12*(9), 42–54.

Yeoh, S. L., Sim, B. L., Tan, Y. H., & Jamaludin, S. (2002). *Science Form 1*. Kuala Lumpur, Malaysia: Bakaprep.

Yilmaz, M. (2017). The effect of data-driven learning on EFL students' acquisition of lexico-grammatical patterns in EFL writing. *Eurasian Journal of Applied Linguistics, 3*(2), 75–88.

Yoon, H-J. (2018). The development of ESL writing quality and lexical proficiency: Suggestions for assessing writing achievement. *Language Assessment Quarterly, 15*(4), 387–405.

Zamel, V. (1985). Responding to student writing. *TESOL Quarterly, 19*(1), 79–101.

Zareva, A. (2012). Partial word knowledge: Frontier words in the L2 mental lexicon. *International Review of Applied Linguistics in Language Teaching, 50*(4), 277–301.

Zhong, H. (2018). The relationship between receptive and productive vocabulary knowledge: A perspective from vocabulary use in sentence writing. *The Language Learning Journal, 46*(4), 357–370.

Index

academic vocabulary, 2, 8–10, 14, 37–38, 45–46, 50, 60–61, 70; specialized lists, 39. *See also* vocabulary, specialized; word lists, specific domains
Academic Word List, 9, 38, 40–41. *See also* word lists
AccurIT, 93
affixes, 25–26; levels, 26; order of acquisition, 27–28
AntConc, 104, 113
antonyms, 27
AwkChecker, 93

bases. *See* word roots
baseword lists, 107–108
bilingual learners, 3, 116, 122–126, 128
BNC. *See* British National Corpus
BNC/COCA lists, 60–62
book flood approach, 72–73
British Academic Writing in English, 102
British National Corpus, 11, 60–61, 101

Centre for English Corpus Linguistics, 103
COBUILD dictionary, 108
COCA. *See* Corpus of Contemporary American English
codes in error feedback, 95–96
cognates, 24; false, 24–25
collaborative writing, 118
collocations, 12–15, 17, 27, 43, 65, 81, 94–95, 110–111; errors in, 93, 110; identifying, 65
Compleat Lexical Tutor, 105, 113
computer tools. *See* vocabulary learning, technology in
concordance data, 109
concordance lines, 105, 108, 111
context for L2 writing, 34, 39
Controlled Productive Vocabulary Levels Test, 53–54
controlled writing task, 78
core vocabulary, 8, 19
corpora, discipline-specific, 112
corpora, electronic: British Academic Writing in English, 102; British National Corpus, 11, 60–61, 101; Centre for English Corpus Linguistics, 103; Common Language Resources and Technology Infrastructure, 103; Corpus of Contemporary American English, 11, 60–61, 102, 108; Corpus Resource Database, 102; International Corpus of English, 102; International Corpus of Learner English, 102; Michigan Corpus of Upper-level Student Papers, 102; Weisser specialized corpora, 102

corpora, electronic, of texts, 40, 100–103, 111. *See also* data and vocabulary
corpus-based dictionaries, 101
corpus construction guides, 103
Corpus of Contemporary American English, 11, 60–61, 102, 108
Corpus Resource Database, 102

data-driven learning (DDL), 109–112
data and vocabulary, 109
deep processing of vocabulary, 79–80
dictionaries, 4, 32

ecology vocabulary, 11
engineering vocabulary, 40–41
English for Academic Purposes (EAP), 33, 51; collocations list for, 43–44
English for Occupational Purposes, 33
English for Specific Purposes, 33
errors, vocabulary, 88–98; codes to identify, 95–96; with collocations and lexical bundles, 93, 110; formality level, 92; interference from L1, 92; interlingual, 89–90; intralingual, 89–90; online tools to detect, 93, 110; types, 95; underspecification, 92; word choice, 91–92; word length, effect on, 90. *See also* online resources
extensive reading, 72–75

feedback on writing, 94–97, 118
form, in vocabulary knowledge, 17–23, 81
form-meaning relationships, 29–30, 81, 91. *See also* network building, in mental lexicon
formulaic sequences. *See* lexical bundles
frequency of words, 37, 42, 99–100, 110
frontier words, 29–30
function words, 19, 35, 110

General Service List (West), 9, 35–36, 40–41; newer lists, 35
general service words, 8–9, 11, 14, 35–36
Generation 1.5 students, 33–34
Greek and Latin, borrowing from, 22, 24, 90–91

high-frequency words. *See* general service words
hyponyms, 27

idioms, 13, 15
incidental vocabulary acquisition, 74, 76–77
interlanguage, 89
International Corpus of English, 102
International Corpus of Learner English, 102
Involvement Load Hypothesis, 80

K1 and K2 words, 9, 35–36, 40–41, 60, 85–86, 106
Kids 01 to Kids 09 word lists, 107
Kids-250 word lists, 63–64

L1, value of in L2 classroom, 3, 116, 122–124
languages, in L2 classroom, 2–3
learner autonomy, 114–28; and learner differences, 125; and teacher concerns, 118–19, 125
lexical bundles, 12–15, 44–45, 65, 94–95, 110; in academic writing, 45; errors in, 93

lexical chunks. *See* lexical bundles
lexical diversity, 55–59, 65–66
lexical frequency profile, 59
lexical relations, paradigmatic, 27, 54
lexical sophistication, 55, 59–60, 63, 65–66
lexical variation, and writing quality, 13–14, 66
low-frequency words, 10

mapping meaning onto form, 20–21, 23–24
mental lexicon, 17, 27–28
Michigan Corpus of Upper-level Student Papers (MICUSP), 102
MonoConc Pro, 106
morphological regularity, 90
morphology, 91
multilingual learners, 3, 116, 122–126, 128
multiword segments. *See* lexical bundles

Nation (Paul) website, 104
needs analysis, L2 writers, 39
NetCollo, 104, 110–11
network building, in mental lexicon, 27–28
N-Gram, 105
notebooks, vocabulary. *See* vocabulary logs

online collocation explorer, 110
online resources: AccurIT, 93; AntConc, 104, 113; AwkChecker, 93; COBUILD dictionary, 108; Coh-Metrix, 105; Compleat Lexical Tutor, 105, 113; Concordance, 105; NetCollo, 104, 110–11; N-Gram, 105; Paul Nation website, 104; Tool for the Automatic Analysis of Lexical Sophistication, 105; UAM Computer Tools, 104; VocabProfile, 105–6; Web-Based L2 Syntactic Complexity Analyzer, 104; Word and Phrase, 104
orthographic regularity, 90

phraseology. *See* lexical bundles
polysemy, 21
portfolio writing, 81–82
power, role in L2 classroom, 3, 118
prefixes, 21–24, 31, 90. *See also* affixes
productive skills, 17, 54, 68–87; plateau effect and, 69
pushed output activities, 79–83, 86–87

reading and writing relationship, 77–78, 83
receptive-productive relationship, 70–71
receptive skills, 17, 54, 70
Romance languages, roots, 22

science vocabulary: high school, 41–42, 47–49; university, 42
self-directed learners. *See* learner autonomy
semantically related pairs. *See* collocations
semantic transparency, 22
Semitic languages, 22
software programs, 106; MonoConc Pro, 106; VocabProfile, 105–6; WordSmith Tools, 106, 113
spelling, 20–21
student-centered classroom. *See* learner autonomy
subject-dependent words, 10
subject-independent words, 9–10, 38

sub-technical words. *See* academic vocabulary
suffixes, 21–23, 31. *See also* affixes
synformy, 91
synonyms, 27, 83
syntagmatic relations, 27, 54

TAALES, 105
target vocabulary engagement, 76–79, 119
target words, 94
teacher and learner roles, 2, 115, 117
technical words, 2, 8–10, 14, 35–36, 40, 45–46, 51; in subject areas, 36–37. *See also* vocabulary, specialized
textbooks, 6–9
text length and TTR, 59
textual enhancement, 75
translanguaging, 3, 122–124, 128
type-token ratio (TTR), 58–59

UAM Computer Tools, 104

verb choice, 118
VocabProfile, 105–106
vocabulary acquisition in L1, 6
vocabulary cards, 119–120. *See also* vocabulary logs
vocabulary development, direct approach in, 76–77; partial-to-precise continuum, 89, 94
vocabulary in disciplines, 111–12, 127
vocabulary knowledge: breadth, 16–17; depth, 16, 19–20, 54, 83; meaning in, 17–18, 22–23; sampling methods in tests, 54; and use, 17–18
Vocabulary Knowledge Scale, 54–55
vocabulary learning, conditions favoring, 78–79; continuum in, 28–29, 71, 89, 94; explicit, 71, 75; gap in, 39; implicit, 71; input-based effects, 75–76; task-based effects in, 75–76; technology in, 99–113; 4-3-2 activity, 79
Vocabulary Levels Test, 53–54
vocabulary logs, 121–122, 125
vocabulary size: and affix knowledge, 25–26; contemporary English, 6; measuring, 5–6, 52–67; receptive vs. productive, 69; role in writing quality, 13–15, 17
vocabulary, specialized, 7–8, 10, 40

Web-Based L2 Syntactic Complexity Analyzer, 104
web-based resources. *See* online resources
Weisser specialized corpora, 102
Word and Phrase, 104
Word Associates Test, 54
word dispersion, 42
word families, 6–7, 25, 31, 37, 41, 43, 107
word frequency, 37, 42, 99–100, 110
word lists: Academic Word List, 9, 38, 40–41; baseword lists, 107–8; General Service List, 9, 35–36, 40–41; Kids 01 to Kids 09, 107; Kids-250, 63–64; science, 42; specific domains, 45–46
word range and uniformity, 37–38, 42
word roots, 22–24, 31
WordSmith Tools, 106, 113